I Was a Child of Holocaust Survivors

Riverhead Books

a member of

Penguin Group (USA) Inc.

New York

2006

I Was a Child of
Holocaust Survivors

Bernice Eisenstein

RIVERHEAD BOOKS
Published by the Penguin Group
Penguin Group (USA) Inc., 375 Hudson Street, New York, New York 10014,
USA · Penguin Group (Canada), 90 Eglinton Avenue East, Suite 700, Toronto,
Ontario M4P 2Y3, Canada (a division of Pearson Penguin Canada Inc.) · Penguin
Books Ltd, 80 Strand, London WC2R 0RL, England · Penguin Ireland, 25 St
Stephen's Green, Dublin 2, Ireland (a division of Penguin Books Ltd) · Penguin
Group (Australia), 250 Camberwell Road, Camberwell, Victoria 3124, Australia (a
division of Pearson Australia Group Pty Ltd) · Penguin Books India Pvt Ltd, 11
Community Centre, Panchsheel Park, New Delhi–110 017, India · Penguin Group
(NZ), Cnr Airborne and Rosedale Roads, Albany, Auckland 1310, New Zealand (a
division of Pearson New Zealand Ltd) · Penguin Books (South Africa) (Pty)
Ltd, 24 Sturdee Avenue, Rosebank, Johannesburg 2196, South Africa

Penguin Books Ltd, Registered Offices: 80 Strand, London WC2R 0RL, England

Previously published in Canada by McClelland & Stewart Ltd.
Copyright © 2006 by Bernice Eisenstein
Drawings © 2006 by Bernice Eisenstein
All rights reserved. No part of this book may be reproduced, scanned, or distributed
in any printed or electronic form without permission. Please do not participate in
or encourage piracy of copyrighted materials in violation of the author's rights.
Purchase only authorized editions.
Library of Congress Cataloging-in-Publication Data
Eisenstein, Bernice, date.
I was a child of Holocaust survivors / Bernice Eisenstein.
p.   cm.
ISBN 1-59448-918-1
1. Eisenstein, Bernice, 1949– Comic books, strips, etc.   2. Jews—Ontario—
Toronto—Biography—Comic books, strips, etc.   3. Children of Holocaust survivors—
Ontario—Toronto—Biography—Comic books, strips, etc.   4. Holocaust survivors—
Ontario—Toronto—Biography—Comic books, strips, etc.   5. Holocaust, Jewish
(1939–1945)—Comic books, strips, etc.   6. Toronto (Ont.)—Biography—
Comic books, strips, etc.   I. Title.

F1059.5.T689J53   2006   2006046222
971.3'54104092—dc22
[B]

Printed in the United States of America
1 3 5 7 9 10 8 6 4 2

This book is printed on acid-free paper. ∞

Text design concept: Michel Vrána, Black Eye Design
Text design and layout: Tania Craan
Jacket design © Tania Craan
Text in thought balloon on back jacket from *Survival in Auschwitz* by Primo Levi

For John, Anna, and Ben
and for Ellen

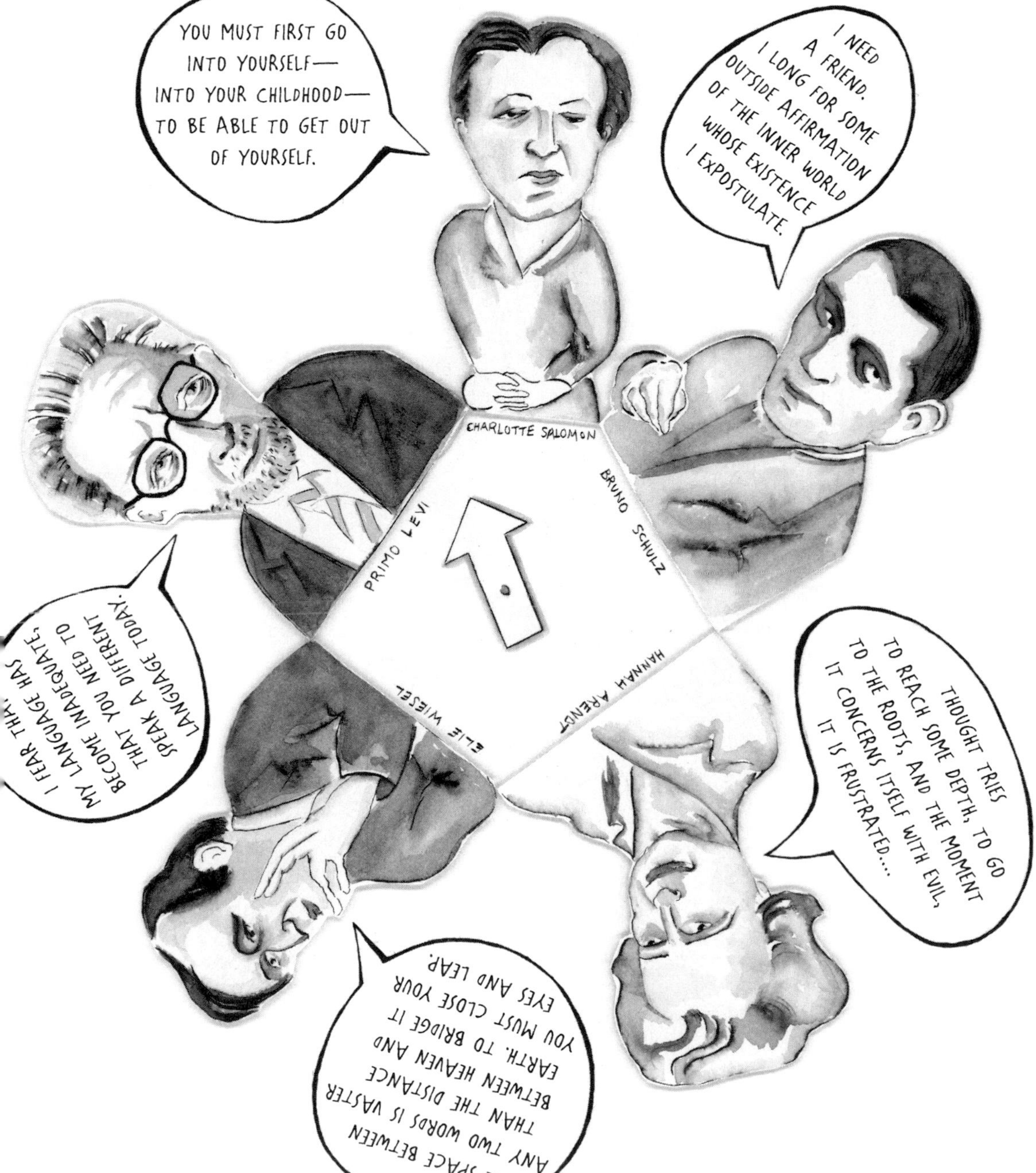
YOU MUST FIRST GO INTO YOURSELF— INTO YOUR CHILDHOOD— TO BE ABLE TO GET OUT OF YOURSELF.
CHARLOTTE SALOMON
I NEED A FRIEND. I LONG FOR SOME OUTSIDE AFFIRMATION OF THE INNER WORLD WHOSE EXISTENCE I EXPOSTULATE.
BRUNO SCHULZ
THOUGHT TRIES TO REACH SOME DEPTH, TO GO TO THE ROOTS, AND THE MOMENT IT CONCERNS ITSELF WITH EVIL, IT IS FRUSTRATED....
HANNAH ARENDT
THE SPACE BETWEEN ANY TWO WORDS IS VASTER THAN THE DISTANCE BETWEEN HEAVEN AND EARTH. TO BRIDGE IT YOU MUST CLOSE YOUR EYES AND LEAP.
ELIE WIESEL
I FEAR THA MY LANGUAGE HAS BECOME INADEQUATE, THAT YOU NEED TO SPEAK A DIFFERENT LANGUAGE TODAY.
PRIMO LEVI

I Was a Child of
Holocaust Survivors

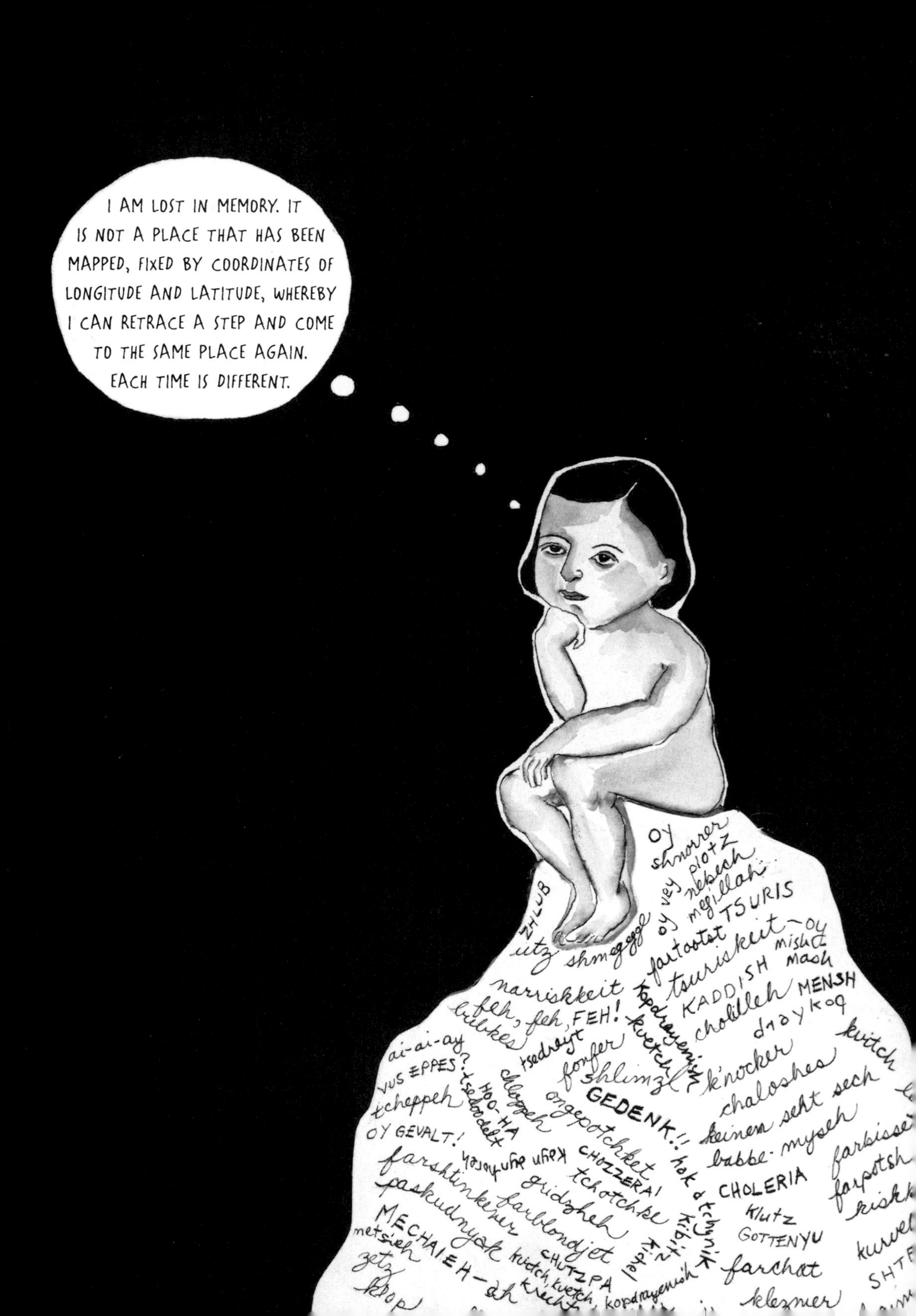

I AM LOST IN MEMORY. IT IS NOT A PLACE THAT HAS BEEN MAPPED, FIXED BY COORDINATES OF LONGITUDE AND LATITUDE, WHEREBY I CAN RETRACE A STEP AND COME TO THE SAME PLACE AGAIN. EACH TIME IS DIFFERENT.
OY
shnorrer
plotz
oy vey
nebech
megillah
ZHLUB
TSURIS
fartootst
shmegeggle
tsuriskeit
KADDISH
MENSH
narriskkeit
feh, feh, FEH!
bubkes
chollileh
kopdrayenish
tsedreyt
kvetch
ai-ai-ay
fonfer
shlimazl
k'nocker
VUS EPPES?
HOO-HA
GEDENK!!
chaloshes
tcheppeh
ongepotchket
keinem seht sech
OY GEVALT!
babbe-myseh
farshtinkener
CHOZZERAI
hak a tchynik
CHOLERIA
tchotchke
gridzheh
paskudnyak
farblondjet
Klutz
GOTTENYU
MECHAIEH
CHUTZPA
farchat
klezmer

The Ring

Death leaves a hole that grows covered with longing.

After my father was buried, I put aside the garment
the rabbi had cut, symbolic of the rending of loss, a black
slip that stays folded away in my dresser. When it was time
to go through my father's clothing, in a closet stuffed full
from years of buying suits and ties and belts and hats,
there were many items to be divided. Most of the clothing
went to charity. I took home several polka-dot ties, wide
ones and thin ones, depending on which era they came
from, and bow ties that needed tying up, not the kind
that simply clipped onto a collar. There was a suede vest
my father always wore when he drove his truck and made
deliveries to people's homes of barbecued chickens and
eggs. I took the vest with me and wore it at times, when

sitting at my desk, delivering ink to paper. And an undershirt, the European kind, sleeveless, low at the neck and back, hanging below my waist, which I used to wear on overheated summer nights when I went to sleep. No strange dark images disturbed those nights.

The thirty days following the burial of the dead is called *shloshim*. It is a time of transition for the mourner as he moves away from the inarticulateness of loss and returns to the familiar rhythm of everyday life. It is a time when memory can fill the hours of night and day. I dreamed often of my father during that first month after his death. He accompanied my sleep. It had been difficult for me to be rid of the final image of his struggle but in my dreams he was always youthful and in good health.

On the eve of the thirtieth day, my father entered a cavelike dwelling and motioned me to him. We held on to each other and then he left. He did not return to my nights for quite some time. Words do not come to fashion themselves around the appearance of my father in that dream, but it is the dream that accompanies me when I draw his face.

Years after my father's death, my mother sold her house and moved into a condominium. It was a practical decision and she carried it out with impressive independence. During a visit to her new home, not long after she had moved, I found her in a closet, going through her jewelry, and she asked me if there were some things that I might want. I have always attached sentiment to possessions, unlike my mother, believing that a person's belongings hold power, can capture the essence of their owner. Perhaps because all the things of value had been taken away from her during the war, my mother is unable to bind herself to any object.

From a little drawstring pouch, she pulled out a ring her father had always worn—small diamonds set in onyx—would I like to have it? I hesitated, not wanting to hurt her feelings. His ring should go to someone who had easy thoughts of warmth whenever he was remembered. No thank you, let someone else have it. Would I like to have something that my grandmother had worn? She presented a ring with a gigantic stone that brought one word to my mind: *chaloshes*, what an eyesore. Once again, but for a different reason, I thought this should go to someone other than myself. After we went through the back-and-forth dance of the giver and the ingrate a few more times, she held out another ring— would I like to have this one?

Rarely has my mother surprised me, but it was hard to believe that she could so casually offer this to me. A plain gold band, not a perfect circle, slightly bent, made oval. My father's wedding ring.

"Now I will tell you its story," she said, and then we sat at her kitchen table with the ring placed between us.

My mother arrived in Canada long before the country became her new home. When she was in Birkenau, she would be marched daily with other female prisoners to a section of the camp named after a country for the abundance it held. For a short while, my mother worked there, in "Canada," in one of the many storehouses. It was a place where the confiscated possessions of Jews were sorted—watches, shoes, clothing, books, kettles, bedding, eyeglasses—separated into piles that constantly grew. Inmates became archaeologists, cataloguing the remnants of their dying culture.

One day, my mother was so cold she found the nerve to ask the guard if she could take a coat from the heap of so many, wear it just for the duration of her work duty. The guard nodded and gestured towards the pile of clothing.

My mother put the coat on and slid her hands into the pockets so as to have the luxury of momentary warmth. Inside, she felt something sewn into the lining, and without attracting any attention to herself, she managed to slip out of its hiding place a ring—this golden ring she was giving to me now.

She hid the ring in her shoe and was able to keep it until the end of the war. It was the ring she gave to my father when they married, not long after Liberation. It was all that she had to give him and he wore it forever. It belongs to my image of him as he lay dying.

The ring has an inscription—L.G. 25/II 14. A man had been married in February 1914, and had died in Auschwitz.

I once read that the Chinese treasure jade because it is believed that the spirit of the wearer enters the stone and can be passed on to the next person. So, from a stranger to my mother, to my father as her gift to him, then to me, I wear the ring as a bittersweet inheritance.

My mother has always been able to give and receive the simpleness of touch, and I hold her in my arms and say thank you. I don't know if she truly comprehends what this gift has meant to me. For reasons that I'm not sure I understand fully myself, I have never been able to form the words between us to explain it.

My father has come back to me, and I carry the spirits of the dead within a circle of gold. The ring holds all that I have come from.

While my father was alive, I searched to find his face among those documented photographs of survivors of Auschwitz—actually, photos from any camp would do. I thought that if I could see him staring out through barbed wire, I would then know how to remember him, know what he was made to become, and then possibly know what he might have been. All my life, I have looked for more in order to fill in the parts of my father that had gone missing, and now the ring that I wear encircles that space, replacing absence with memory.

REGINA

BEN

I have had to create their shadows for myself. The crisp lines they drew had no answers until all that remained was my mother, left behind alone and unmoored. Vague without his definite anger. The Jewish version of Catherine & Heathcliff...

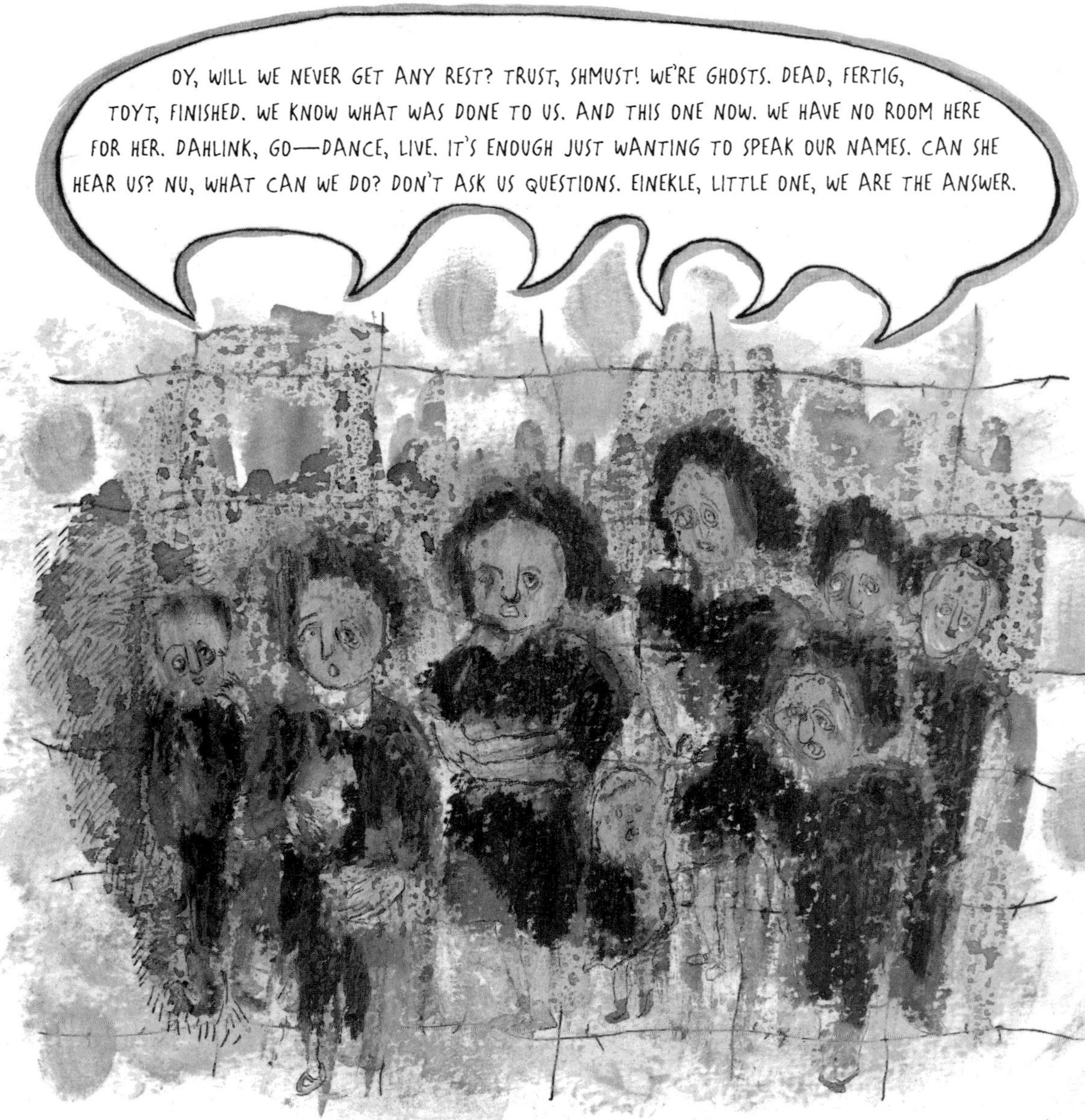
OY, WILL WE NEVER GET ANY REST? TRUST, SHMUST! WE'RE GHOSTS. DEAD, FERTIG, TOYT, FINISHED. WE KNOW WHAT WAS DONE TO US. AND THIS ONE NOW. WE HAVE NO ROOM HERE FOR HER. DAHLINK, GO—DANCE, LIVE. IT'S ENOUGH JUST WANTING TO SPEAK OUR NAMES. CAN SHE HEAR US? NU, WHAT CAN WE DO? DON'T ASK US QUESTIONS. EINEKLE, LITTLE ONE, WE ARE THE ANSWER.

Without the Holocaust

I am lost in memory. It is not a place that has been mapped, fixed by coordinates of longitude and latitude, whereby I can retrace a step and come to the same place again. Each time is different.

With senses closed now to the movement of the world that pulls me forward, I am in the basement of our house. It is 1961 and I am eleven years old. Adolf Eichmann is on trial in Israel and in our rec room, with my parents and several of their friends seated in chairs. I had always known that my parents were survivors of the Holocaust, but there is nowhere for

I WORRY THAT THEY WILL BE ANGRY WITH ME AND THINK I HAVE STOLEN THEIR SOULS THAT HAVE ALREADY BEEN STOLEN AWAY. CAN I BE TRUSTED TO LOOK INTO MY HEART AND FIND THEIRS?

me to locate when or how I first became aware of it. As a child, I had somehow absorbed the fact, yet until today its relationship to me had remained invisible. I am standing at the back of the room and it is dark except for the glow of the television. Pictures of skeletal bodies piled one on top of another are on the screen, and suddenly I am injected with the white-heat rush of a new reality.

The Holocaust is a drug and I have entered an opium den, having been given my first taste for free, innocently, by everyone here. I have only just glimpsed its power, scanning the trail of needle marks on the left forearms of each person in the room. This is when my addiction takes hold. My very own monkey on my back. I will discover that there is no end to the dealers I can find for just one more hit, one more entry into a hallucinatory world of ghosts.

My parents don't even realize that they are drug dealers. They could never imagine the kind of high H gives. The way it makes me want to dive into its endless depths, sending me out of my home alone to the cinema, to the library, where I can see every movie and read every book that deals the Holocaust. Reels of film, along with printed pages from books, could all be chopped up into a fine powder, laid down, row upon row, and snorted. When I was in my twenties, André Schwarz-Bart's novel *The Last of the Just* was inhaled three times, just so that I could have the same hit over and over again, leading me to the supreme all-time transcendence of Primo Levi, who left me nodded out, under my bed, curled up in fetal position, still quivering for more.

Often enough, literature permutated into film, and I could float from one right into the other. *Sophie's Choice* the novel became *Sophie's Choice* the movie. I remember that after I saw it, I left the theater, my judgment impaired, and went directly to visit my father with barely enough time to come down from the film's hold over me. I arrived, eyes swollen and red from crying. My father took one look at me and asked what had happened. At the time, I had forgotten that when my parents *did* go to see a Holocaust film, their primary goal was to search the screen for authenticity, to make sure the enactment of events was correctly portrayed. They somehow managed to leave the theater emotionally intact. After I described the movie to my father, he had only one question: Why would you want to see something that did this to you?

Because it's there was all I could say, sounding like Edmund Percival Hillary responding to why he climbed Mount Everest. Because I wanted to see a replication of Auschwitz and be able to imagine my mother and father standing in the background among the other starving inmates. In that way, I thought I could find them. Because, just because— a child's answer to a parent's question.

Because I am your child—someone who learned there was no limit to how much you can socially trade on this stuff: Hey man, I'm different than you are. My parents were in Auschwitz. What do you have that can top that one? I knew I could throw that line out anywhere, anytime—in a sandbox, for instance. Can I play with your shovel and pail? No? Well, my parents were in Auschwitz. . . . At recess: Stop pulling my pigtails because my parents were in Auschwitz. . . . In high school

English class, Arthur Miller's *Death of a Salesman* provided me with a battle cry: "Attention must be paid"—not only to Willy Loman but to the Holocaust, because my parents . . . Backpacking in Europe, the heaviest part of my baggage was my parents' history, and the Europeans I met were receptive to being informed of it every time I unpacked. Out on dates: I'm not like the other girls you date because my parents . . . Making friends feel privileged to know me once I had confided that—at this point, fill in the missing chorus. . . . And in and out of one marriage, then finally into another,

> HEY, WAIT! WHICH IS IT? THOU SHALT NOT TAKE ITS NAME IN VAIN OR NOT TAKE IT INTO A VEIN? HELP ME OUT.

with the unspoken need to be loved even more because my parents were in Auschwitz.

It was the paragon of non sequiturs, and I would trade on its cachet, shamelessly it seems to me now, with a mixed bag of reasons and emotions—in order for the attention to be paid to me. It was a way of staking claim to my position in the world—a black-and-white perspective, verging on color blindness. Don't get me wrong. It wasn't as if every moment, every conversation, every encounter,

revolved around the Holocaust. There were minutes, days, months, when my addiction subsided, crawled back into my skin, and I had no need to see The Man for another dose. But the craving is there, it is always there. I'm tied to it.

As my parents and their friends sat before a television set in Canada and listened to Eichmann speak to them, his witnesses and jurors, I felt them whisper to me, "Never forget." Those words, mixed into a syringe's heady cocktail, not only overtook me in a dark room in our basement, they were injected into the world: Attention must be paid. So the big conundrum, for me, is that those two words were declared by a group of people who, in order for their New World lives to be made, must have needed to forget. But, inevitably, as those lives have unfolded, at any occasion for celebration— at births, bar mitzvahs, weddings, Jewish holidays— joy is always accompanied with an undercurrent of loss.

While growing up and trying to discover my own way into the world, I sometimes found it impossible not to wander off course, with a different aim in mind. Knowing that the Holocaust happened was not enough, I needed to know what it had done to my parents. I'd follow the winding road of their sketched-in pasts, and more often than not ended up at the Lost and Found.

"Just what exactly are you looking for? Be quick, there are many more behind you in the line."

"I want to find my father's and mother's eyes, looking out from behind barbed wire. You know, like in the famous photo that Margaret Bourke-White took, the one in *Life* magazine, with all the concentration camp victims. I want to compare those eyes to the ones I know."

"Why? Sounds more like something they lost, not you. Why don't you send your parents instead, and then I'll see what I can do. Next . . ."

He doesn't understand that's why I'm here. I've lost something I've never had. Besides, my parents would be confused to see me standing here, as a child, as a teenager, as an adult. But I keep returning with the same question I've always had, from that first moment while watching Eichmann's trial on television: Where are my parents' eyes?

There is no Holocaust Anonymous to go to, no Ten-Commandment Step Program, no audience to stand before and state, "Hello, everyone. I am addicted to the Holocaust. Today is my first day of being clean and I don't need the Holocaust anymore to feel like a worthy person." And if there were such a thing, I'm convinced that I would be interrupted, mid-confession, as heavy doors at the back of the room are pushed open and my father and my mother appear, asking me in unison, *Why are you here?* Great! Now I'm speechless, unable to continue. What could I possibly say to help them both understand other than, Because I will *always* be your child.

Where does that leave me now—evicted by my parents' concern from an illusory place during a fabricated meeting of an organization whose initials form the word HA . . . ?

There's no end to how far an obsessed imagination can run with all of this. Yet to rid myself of this habit, this calling, I would have to blind my eyes, cover my ears, seal my lips, and erase the truth that without the Holocaust I would not be who I am. It has seared and branded me with its stippled mark on my forearm and pulled me into its world, irrevocably, as its offspring. The collective memory of a generation speaks and I am bound to listen, see its horrors, and feel its outrage.

When the judge presiding over the Eichmann trial addressed the Israeli court, he said "that in order to punish the accused and deter others, the maximum penalty laid down in the law must be imposed on him." I knew from that day on that I had been sentenced as well.

Growing New Skin

Watch the passing of a life and the moment strips the skin of the observer. In that instant, an entire world dies. Nothing is familiar. How is one able to regain connection, belonging, when all that was as innocent as being alive has been taken away?

My parents arrived in a new country draped in loss, with their memories deprived of the ability to offer comfort. In time, memory is soothed, if never fully healed. A second skin covers over and they become familiar to themselves once more.

Even though the past was something my parents tried to keep at a distance from their children, out of harm's reach, it inevitably shadowed the landscape in which we would grow.

I am fourteen years old when a long-distance call at three o'clock in the morning wakes up our sleeping household. I answer the phone. A man from Australia is looking for my father. "Does Barek . . . Ben Eisenstein live there?" I hand the receiver to my father, who is by now standing beside me. There is a brief conversation in Yiddish. Something about a pair of boots.

After, there is a story to tell us. This man from Australia had been trying to locate my father for almost twenty years, since the end of the war, to let him know that, because of him, he had survived the death march out of Auschwitz, just before the camp was liberated in 1945. The man had been chosen to go on the march and it was clear that he would not be able to survive if he did not have proper boots. My father had stolen a pair of boots and given them to this man, who was now calling to thank him and to say that he was alive, living in Australia, and with a family. Their conversation passed quickly, ending with a Yiddish farewell, *zei gezunt*, be well, and with those words the unsettled path of one man's debt to another found its way back to its source.

That night, for the first time, I felt my father within his own past. But I had no chronology, no laid-out sequence of events, in order for me to hold a newly found fragment and place it where it belonged.

After my father died, I wore his dotted ties, his suede vest, and I sewed buttons into the waistband of my pants for his suspenders. I easily conjured up his presence.

His vision, from the constantly passing bars,
has grown so weary that it cannot hold
anything else. It seems to him there are
a thousand bars, and behind the bars, no world.

As he paces in cramped circles, over and over,
the movement of his powerful soft strides
is like a ritual dance around a center
in which a mighty will stands paralyzed.

It seems as if Rilke knew my father long before I did, clothing his essence in words. Always, my father reminded me of a caged animal: a panther, sleek and mysterious with the elegant sheen of its fur. Forever pacing inside his cage. Silent, but in continual motion. When he was angry, which seemed often, the veins of my father's neck would bulge, promising to burst at any given moment. By today's measure, he would not be considered a tall man, but for his generation, at five feet nine inches, he was. He was lithe and athletic. The sound of his footstep left no echo. Age had done nothing to alter his hairline and his thick black hair was always swept back dramatically. Only the length of his sideburns, long or short, marked the passage of time, with the final interruption of gray. And his clothes—if closets were built to contain everything a person had worn throughout his lifetime, my father's would have been gargantuan, complete with a revolving tie rack. Fat ties, skinny ties, polka-dotted ties, large white dots against black, large red dots against black, silk, silk, silk, bow ties—for those formal occasions—wide bow ties, skinny bow ties, suspenders, suspenders with button holes, suspenders with clips, black, brown, red ones. I can see him now, coming down the stairs once he was dressed, with his hand to his neck, making the final adjustment to his tie. "How do I look?"

You look great, Dad. You always did.

But like a well-tailored gangster. I remember watching Martin Scorsese's movie *Casino*. The moment Robert De Niro entered a scene wearing a powder-blue leisure suit, clashing plaid shirt, topped off with a garishly colored tie, I thought the film's designer must have approached the ghost of my father and hired him onto the set as costume adviser. And I find myself thinking: Gee, De Niro looks great.

My father's clothes were important to him. I can't recall ever seeing a wrinkle come near him. Let's just cut to the chase and call him dapper, with all the personal pride he must have felt when he looked in the mirror.

Because he was beautiful. His eyes were clear and blue-gray. How I wished to have inherited that color. An expansive brow, a small defining cleft in his chin, and generously fleshed lips. There was always a ferocity in his gaze, luminous through an invisible darkness. *"Keinem seht sech."* No one sees oneself. This was his mantra, and it vibrated throughout the years of growing up in his house. It was his Yiddish nonpareil and it punctuated every argument we had, substituting for his inability to say more. And what didn't we fight over: the friends

I kept, the length of a hemline, the style of my clothing, my use of the car, the state of the world, drugs, laughing at the dinner table (go figure), the fact that I preferred to read in my bedroom throughout the summer as opposed to going outside to suntan—nothing and everything. As he paced within his cage in the rooms of his house, the movement of anyone around him seemed to create ripples of tension that made him snap, crackle, and pop.

When my father sat down at the supper table, no matter what my mother had placed before him—a lamb chop, a piece of broiled chicken, a breaded veal cutlet, some boiled potatoes and vegetables— he would lean in close and then sniff. The plate of food would be pushed away, a look of displeasure on his face, and he'd say, *"Shmeckt avek"*—literally, it smells away— conveying that the food was not found to be appealing. Every dinnertime, there was this ritual, but eventually my father would proceed to eat. The dodginess and cunning of the Yiddish language is such that the very same phrase, spoken in softer tones, is used when a compliment is given. It could have happened in our home that a guest, smelling the aroma rising from the plate my mother had just placed before him, would look up with pleasure and declare, *"Shmeckt avek."*

My mother, accustomed to the habit of my father's dyspeptic mealtime mood, might defend her cooking, or just accept the criticism, admitting her own fatigue after working all day. Often, she would simply dismiss it with a shrug. Whatever her response was, we all rolled our eyes and then carried on with our meal. I find myself wondering now if my father's behavior was preparation for the indigestion he expected as a result of his ulcer or was it a daily reminder to us—and perhaps to himself—that he had no appetite because of what life had placed before him.

   After supper, my father would rise from the table and go to his bedroom to watch sports or westerns on television—how he

loved those westerns—or head off to one of his many all-night poker games.

"I'd lie down in front of a truck for you" was another one of my father's familiar phrases, a statement of his desire to sacrifice himself, if necessary, to be a shield for those he loved. I had heard this said so often that I sometimes expected the event, looking over my shoulder for that truck to come tearing down the road, speeding out of control. I never doubted the fierce love my father had for me, but there were times when I longed for a simpler, less heroic, expression of it. An openness or curiosity about what I was thinking or what my interests were. A conversation to have with him beyond declarations.

Perhaps then he might have trusted that I could find my own way in what he knew to be a difficult world.

When he pronounced his feelings, my father did so with either few words or quick motion, but their aftershock still remains.

I remember when I moved back to Toronto from England, having lived abroad for three years, I stayed briefly at my parents' house until I was able to find an apartment. I returned with a few new possessions—rocks with fossils, dried flowers, polished agates, rusted coils, and shells. They were small items of no value to anyone other than myself, things that had caught my eye, which I had picked up and put into my pocket. If it is impossible for the truth to be held in one's pocket, I always filled my own with objects that could facilitate passage to a place and a time. One night I brought my father a box containing porcelain-thin crab shells wrapped in tissue. I thought that they might help me describe to him a beach I had explored when I had visited Scotland. I laid them out, and then, without a word, he crushed them, angry. It was an ugly moment and I left the room, reduced to fragments myself. Several days later I found an apartment and moved.

Once I had relocated, my father came to visit, along with my mother and my brother, Michael. It was a difficult time in my life—I was twenty-seven, and had recently ended a marriage. We were having tea, the four of us seated at the kitchen table. My father sat quietly for a while and then he told me that sometimes a parent has a special feeling for a child and that that is what he always had for me. Michael heard his words, yet the two of us knew their meaning did not lessen what existed between father and son.

Swift anger and then this, another touchstone, both emotions framing my father as a way for me to understand him as my parent. Enraged at my fragility, that I could become attached to things of small consequence, when his own attachments had disappeared. As the parent he became because he could not save his own.

My father has been dead now for longer than a decade. I cannot turn to him and tell him that I have learned to discern his spilled-out fury and expressions of love as one and the same. He is no longer here for me to discover his past, to ask him about the war, about Auschwitz, or what life was like growing up in Poland. About his family, his parents, my grandparents. Though from early on, I knew that the past was something not to be ventured into. I had learned from the handful of times I had asked. My father could only begin to answer with a few willing words and then stop. He would cry. Sitting in silence beside him, I did not want to make him go further. I was left to find the pieces of his past, led by the wish to have more.

I can still hear his staccato bursts of English-Yiddish, but I cannot ask him: Who will now promise to lie down in front of a truck for me? I am left with the inked-in shapes of line and word to trace his movement, his anger, his love.

Barek (Beryl) Eisenstein was born in Miechow, Poland, in 1917. His father and mother were named Mordechai (Motel) and Sarah (Surela). He had two sisters, Bina (Binche) and Hannah (Chana), and a brother, Jacob (Yakov).

He had been conscripted into the Polish cavalry and when war broke out in 1939, Ben fought on the western side of the country not far from Warsaw. When his horse was wounded, he separated from his regiment and he walked to Warsaw, continuing on back home to Miechow, to his family. A few days after Poland was invaded, the German army entered Miechow. By November 1940, twenty-five hundred Jews were enclosed in a ghetto there. Soon after, Ben and Jacob found themselves among a group of men who had been selected by the Germans and taken from Miechow to a military base outside of Cracow, where they were forced into labor until the base was disassembled nearly two years later. During that time, even as conditions grew worse in the ghetto, Ben was sometimes able to make contact with his family. When he learned that his sister Binche had married and was pregnant, he went to the German officer in charge and asked if arrangements could be made to bring his family to the base. He was told that a pregnant woman was not allowed, and Ben's father refused to leave with his wife and Chana and let Binche and her husband remain behind. Not long afterwards, Ben and Jacob learned that the Miechow ghetto had been liquidated, that their family was dead. He and Jacob were then sent to Plaszow, a concentration camp that has become well known as a result of the movie based on Thomas Keneally's book *Schindler's Ark*. Conditions at the camp were intolerable, the lice inescapable. In the two years my father suffered there, selections were routinely made and Jews were moved out of the camp, unaware of their destinations. In 1944, my father was selected, consoled only by the thought that the next place might be different, but he was to become separated from Jacob. A train took my father to Auschwitz.

On arrival, he made fast friends with a group of eight men, an octet of survival, sworn to help one another should any weaken in spirit or fall ill. My father was in Auschwitz for eleven months, right up until Liberation. It was just before this, during the last days of chaos in the camp, that he met my mother. She had avoided the death march many had been sent on and had hidden with a few of her friends until they were discovered by German guards and taken to another area of the camp, close to its entrance, near the gate. The women in the small group were then placed in the camp's brothel. What had once been a building in which soldiers were offered pleasure became the last place of confinement for my mother. It was here that my parents first met. My father and his friends had come to protect the women from harm as the Russian Red Army approached and many German soldiers, desperate in defeat, were fleeing. This is when my father and mother's life together began.

Like Adam and Eve, ousted from a perverted Eden, they were cast out to find another home. Who would later bless their union, to stand witness to the joining together of their lives? On whose ears would these words fall: *I am my beloved's and my beloved is mine*. I will be the canopy over their uncovered heads. I will bear witness to their uniting in sorrow and loss, to have and to hold, protected and anchored by love, until death did part one from the other forty-six years later.

And what is then obliged to the homeless, to the displaced? You take a concentration camp, say Bergen–Belsen

in Germany, and turn it into a large
DP camp for survivors. Thousands will
find their way here. My parents arrive six
months after Liberation. A year later, this
is where my sister, Sharon, will be born
and it will be my parents' home until,
in 1948, they leave Europe. My
father will engage voraciously
in black-marketing, trade
whatever he can and turn
goods into jewels, trying to
amass what he considered
would be enough for life in the
New World. But nothing is enough. Nothing is what they
have. His stones will be stolen from him.

Only weeks after Liberation, my father had found
his way to Katowice, an industrial city in Upper Silesia,
where, along with some other Jews who had left the
camps, he would join the Polish paramilitary. He would
adopt a new name, Bolek Jurkowski, and wear a uniform,
carry a Luger, and seek out collaborators and Nazis, as if
revenge could become graveclothes to cover the bodies
of his father, his mother, his two sisters. His fists would
be clenched and he would hold within himself a silent,
mournful howl that was to stay with him throughout his
life until much later and in a different world, when on
the day before my father dies, the lament in his heart
extinguishes as I stand close to him and he puts his open
hand on my pregnant belly and says that my child will
have his name.

They were called "Greenies," greenhorns, once they arrived in the New World. What color were they before they planted feet on strange ground? Was the land so green that its potent chlorophyll entered their pores and took over, making them appear even more alien than the aliens they were? Think of all that the color green conjures: freshness, growth, rejuvenation, nausea, seasickness, bile—green with envy, green-eyed monsters, Greenies in the Nu World.

This is how my parents, Ben and Regina, came to Toronto, Canada, in 1948: sprayed green by order of government officials. In this way, they could be once again identified. They were sent out as The Thing from the sludge swamp of Europe, and waited to see what would sprout from their coat of one color.

My father sprouted feathers, soft fluffy chicken feathers. He set up shop in Kensington Market, in Toronto, and became a kosher butcher.

The store was narrow and

dimly lit, with an old butcher
block for carving, cutting, and
wrapping up chicken parts.
At the back, there was a large
walk-in refrigerator. He also
sold fish, whitefish and carp,
making sure his customers
always had ample amounts for
their gefilte fish. It was a sight
to see him scale a carp. They
were kept live in a large tank
in the dank subterrain of the
basement. He would bring a
fish up, place it on the white
marble counter, and then
proceed to swiftly and expert-
ly scale and gut, the large
iridescent scales flying
around the room, circling
his head like shooting stars.

What thoughts filled his
mind during all those years as a
kosher butcher, in his shop and
when he drove a truck to make
deliveries to neighboring
homes? Did he daydream himself
into his youth, with his parents
and siblings, in Miechow, before
the war? Would he allow the
silence of remembering what he

could not voice to take him out of his routine, delivering chickens, chickens, and returning to the shop for the plucking of more freshly butchered chickens. Chickens that would be cut up into serving parts, wrapped in waxed brown paper, ready for another delivery, ready to be brought home to our table.

If my father never managed to get rich, at least his family would never go without chicken. How we ate that chicken! In soup, barbecued, boiled, broiled, crisp-skinned, sweet and succulent. And tagged. Kosher chickens have a metal clip attached to their skin, signifying that they've been properly butchered according to the rules of the rabbinate. At each meal, the one who got the portion with the tag felt lucky, as if he had just pulled out the prize in a box of Cracker Jack.

But as hard as my parents worked together in the store, through long hours and days, my father still managed to find time to play poker. He was a card player, a *korten shpiler*, a rounder, a gambler. He loved holding five cards in his hand, slapping them down on the table for a draw, putting money in the pot, winning and losing. He had never finished high school but he knew the numbers, played the odds. After one card was placed face up on the table, he would know exactly what was in everyone else's hand. He could count columns of numbers quicker than anyone I ever saw, and he played cards everywhere. On the days when my mother did not go to work with him, my father would hold a game with three other men in a small room at the back of the shop. Shh—don't tell Mommy.

It was his excitement for gambling that led my father to
scoop me up with a couple of friends on our street and take
us to the grounds of the Canadian National Exhibi-
tion one day in the summer I was seven. We didn't go
on any rides—I hated them anyway, nausea rose rapidly—
but we all arrived home, well after the sun had set,
weighted down with every prize there was to be won:
stuffed animals ranging from small, furry, and cuddly to
ungraspably large and dominant, and budgie birds for all,
cages included, of course. My father had found his game:
tossing dimes onto a plate, and don't think it was easy.
The plates were greased, probably with *shmaltz*, chicken fat,
so that the dimes would hit the surface and slide right off,
making most players reach into their pockets for another
try, and another. . . . I remember a boy approaching my
father, offering his own dime with the hope that he too
could win a prize. And win he did. Another budgie bird
gets a new home. This time I could tell my mother—the

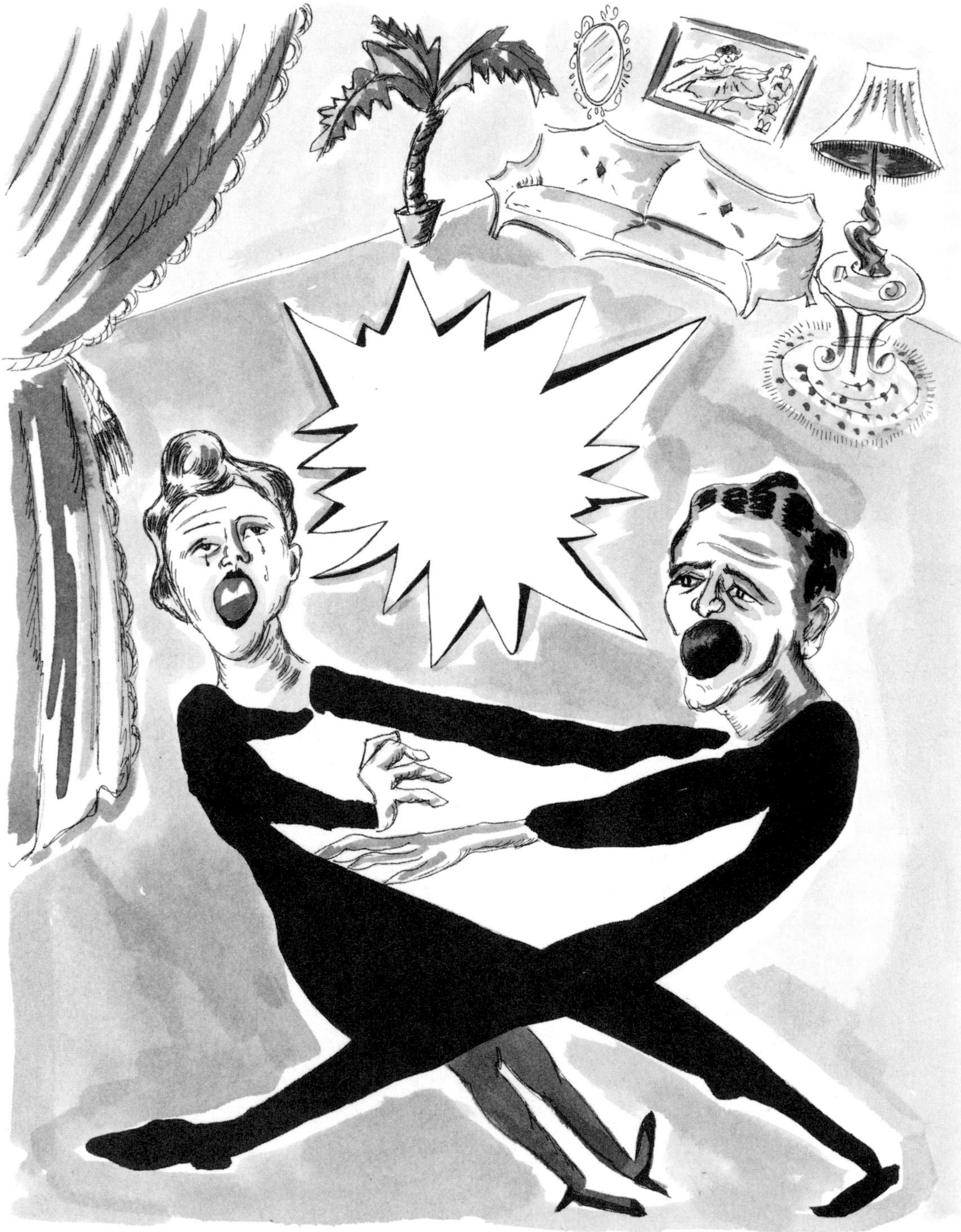

loot was too big to hide. My father also grew larger that day, planting seeds for a legend to grow.

When I was ten, we moved to the suburbs at the north end of the city, and it wasn't long before strangers began to phone. Without ever meeting the face that belonged to the gravelly voice, I could readily see the flattened nose and the fat cigar in a permanent dangle at the side of the mouth.

There were Saturday-night card games with my parents' friends, the Group. A social game. Low ante, high cholesterol. Tuesday- and Thursday-night poker with the Voices. High stakes, high-powered. And by the time I was sixteen, for one full year after he got tired of plucking chickens and sold his business, looking to enter a different trade, my father played all the days of the week in a room at the Westbury Hotel. During that year, there were many telephone calls made by voices pickled in brine, telling my father when to come. If I was ever to take the call, my mother had instructed me not to pass on the message. Shh—don't tell Daddy. My parents fought often, but it reached a pitch that year. I remember one time when my mother locked the front screen door before she went to bed and I was awakened by my father tapping at my bedroom window, wanting me to get up and let him in. With regularity, he came home so late from a poker game that he'd find his family sitting down to breakfast.

I once asked my father if he was a good card player. Overall, he said, he had come out ahead. I never knew the details of the wins or the losses, only the rift his never-ending playing caused between my parents. There were endless arguments over the *korten shpilen*. But in memory, he's enshrined in a Hall of Fame I can visit anytime.

My father had a heart attack when he was fifty-four. The two of us had been engaged in our usual tango—we were fighting. Over the years, whether it was laughing when he preferred quiet, being quiet when he wanted an answer, disagreeing when he wanted agreement—whatever—I had never been able to figure out exactly what spark I provided to ignite him. But this time he clutched his chest. He was always dramatic and many *oy*s dotted the air, so it was hard to figure out why this night was different from any other night. Stop that. Let's fight fair. Don't bring ulcers or hemorrhoids or "*Oy*, you're killing me" into the ring. This bout had the potential for producing months of hair-pulling guilt with a psychiatrist but, call it self-preservation or a moment of clarity, I somehow managed not to implicate myself as Producer of the First Heart Attack. A narrow escape indeed. Luckily, it was only a mild

I DIDN'T FEEL ANY BETTER WHEN I READ THAT THE UNRESOLVED CONFLICT SURVIVORS HAVE WITH AGGRESSION MAKES IT HARD FOR THEIR CHILDREN TO LOOK UP TO THEM AS FIGURES OF AUTHORITY.

attack, but it required a period of recuperative house arrest. So my mother went off to work alone every day to the clothing store they had bought a few years earlier, and she would come home exhausted.

Finally, and for an entire month, my father sat, without stress, concentrated while he played poker in his homegrown casino. Shh—don't tell Mommy.

Every weekday, during his recuperation, a very short man with a leathery face entered our house. His limousine would be parked in the driveway with his bulked-up comic-book bodyguard leaning patiently against the car, waiting several hours till the card game was over.

My father and this stranger faced each other across the kitchen table, rarely speaking. My brother and I—my sister was already married, no longer in the house—were the official members of the Don't Tell Mommy Club with special privileges of dispensation: we were allowed to be mute observers of the action. My father looked healthy, but at every game he wore a robe, silk, over his pajamas, giving him the appearance of the housebound patient he was supposed to be. Between the hours after we arrived home from school and my mother's return from work, my father and this man played five-card stud, two hundred dollars per ante, and from there the sky was the limit. What did I know? I just watched in amazement. So this was my father at his best, engrossed in an activity he loved, utterly at ease, focused, and still. There he was, resembling a successful small-time hood right out of some Jewish Damon Runyon pulp novel, being silently cheered on by his offspring. My father sat, contained in the present, no thought given to revenge, to plucking chickens or selling women's clothing, at peace in his modernized suburban *shtetl*.

And he won and he kept winning—heart attacks must be good luck for a gambler.
Years later, and some time after my father died, I wandered into a neighborhood bakery. The area was long past being filled primarily with Jewish immigrants, but this store was a dwindling holdout. I was talking to the owner, who, perhaps recognizing something about my face, asked who my father was. When I told him, without hesitation, he responded, "Too bad your father loved playing cards so much, your family might have had some money." His crude directness caught me off guard and I lost the moment to rise to my father's defense: he left me rich with his passion.

Like a dusty book in a reference library, memory gets pulled off the shelf and riffled through to find a familiar passage to look at once more. Often when I think of my father, I picture him stretched out on his bed, one arm behind his head, a hand in his pocket, watching westerns on television. I don't think that he had favorites, he loved them all.

Why? I used to wonder. What release did they provide for him? Where did they take him to after a long day of work, preparing orders of chickens, eggs, fish, alongside his wife, and later, in the clothing business, this time adding feathers to clientele, selling dresses to women? What did this man, this transplanted tenderfoot from Poland, understand as he watched John Wayne and Montgomery Clift head 'em up and move 'em out across the cinematic plains? Where did my father go when he rode out across the Wild West?

Didn't he feel uncomfortable, have a Yiddish sense of déjà vu, been there, done that, as he passed under the bowed entranceway to the OK Corral, his horse hesitating for a moment, refusing to go farther? Giddyup . . .

Over and over again in this dusty frontier, standing up to the rustlers, the corrupt sheriff, the frightened townsfolk, he wasn't in Tombstone, he was back in a different past. Only here, lying in bed watching television, could he stand alongside his heroes. There was never a question as to evil being vanquished. Good beat Evil. This was paradise and the rules were simple. Stand up to the enemy, shoot him down, save the town, and you'll never need to look back.

Alone, out of the East, he rides into Auschwitz, slowly passing through the archway. He gets off his horse and ties it up to barbed wire. There is no one in sight, the streets are bare. Yup, it's time to *arbeit* and finally *macht* everyone *frei*. He sniffs the air and says, *"Shmeckt avek."* A storm threatens the sky and thunder cracks, lightning strikes the ground where he is standing. Out of nowhere, Nazis appear before him. Surrounded, he is outnumbered. But he is calm, his hand steady, and his gaze resolute upon the enemy.

The moment is still, a universe suspended in a freeze-frame. Wind that carries smoke rising from the chimneys of crematoriums stops. The prisoners in their barracks are motionless, their breath unable to escape. There is no silver bullet, no smoke from a gun, no bloodshed. Judgment Day is here.

He stands before them and unleashes a moan so powerful that its resonance causes tremors in the ground upon which he stands, and with its fierceness the earth splits, swallowing the Nazis whole. Sent to the underworld, they are imprisoned in the earth's core, which will now and for eternity beat a rhythmic pulse of remembrance to guide the report of the winds.

Quietly my father goes from barrack to barrack, opening the doors, his footsteps soundless. The prisoners shield their eyes from the light as they wander out to the courtyard where they had been pulled from the hands of their mothers, their fathers, their sisters, brothers, their children, from all who had been herded to the left.

It has taken a nightmare to imagine how things are meant to be. And in this imagining, I see my father.

You look good, Dad. You always did.

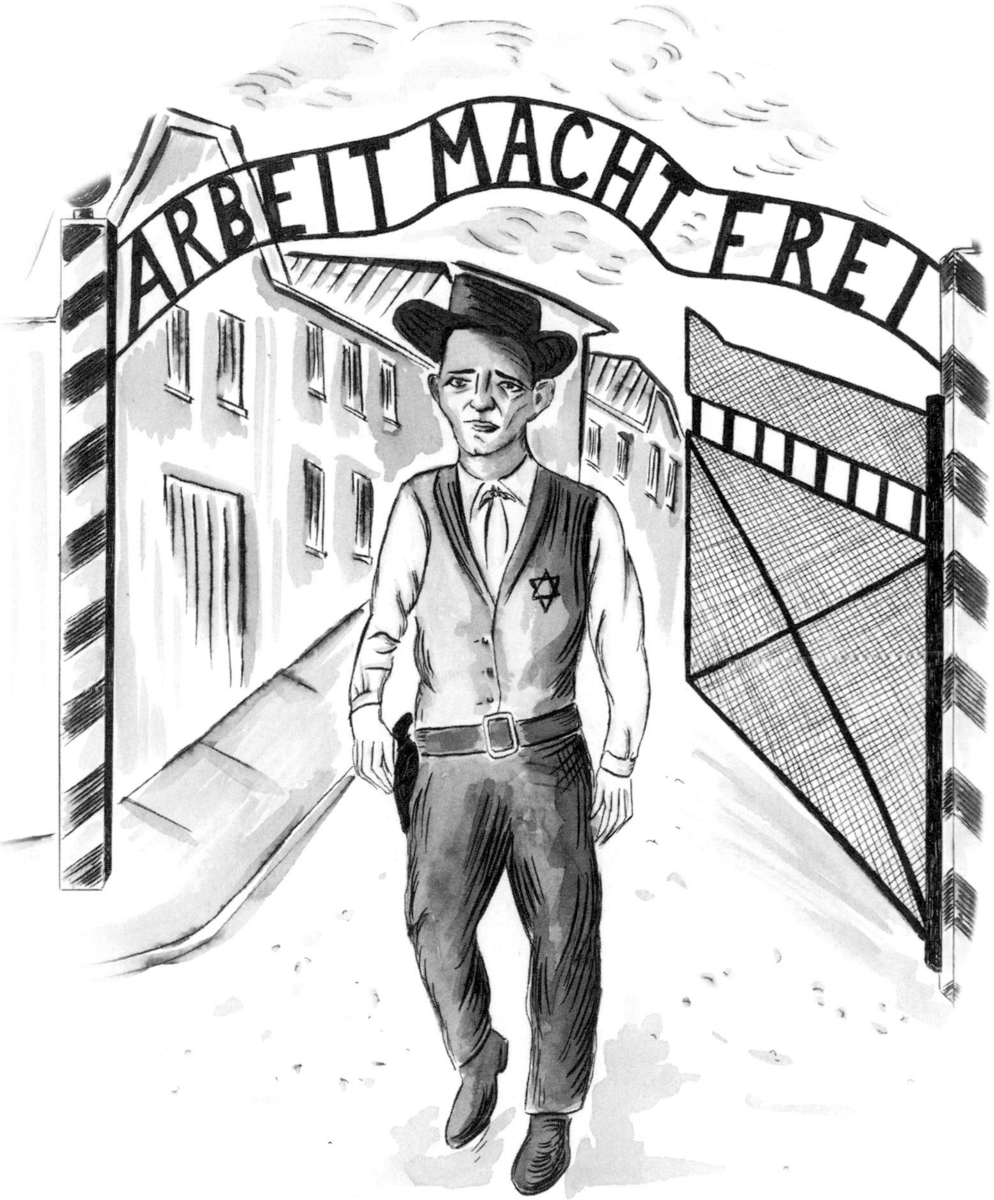
ARBEIT MACHT FREI

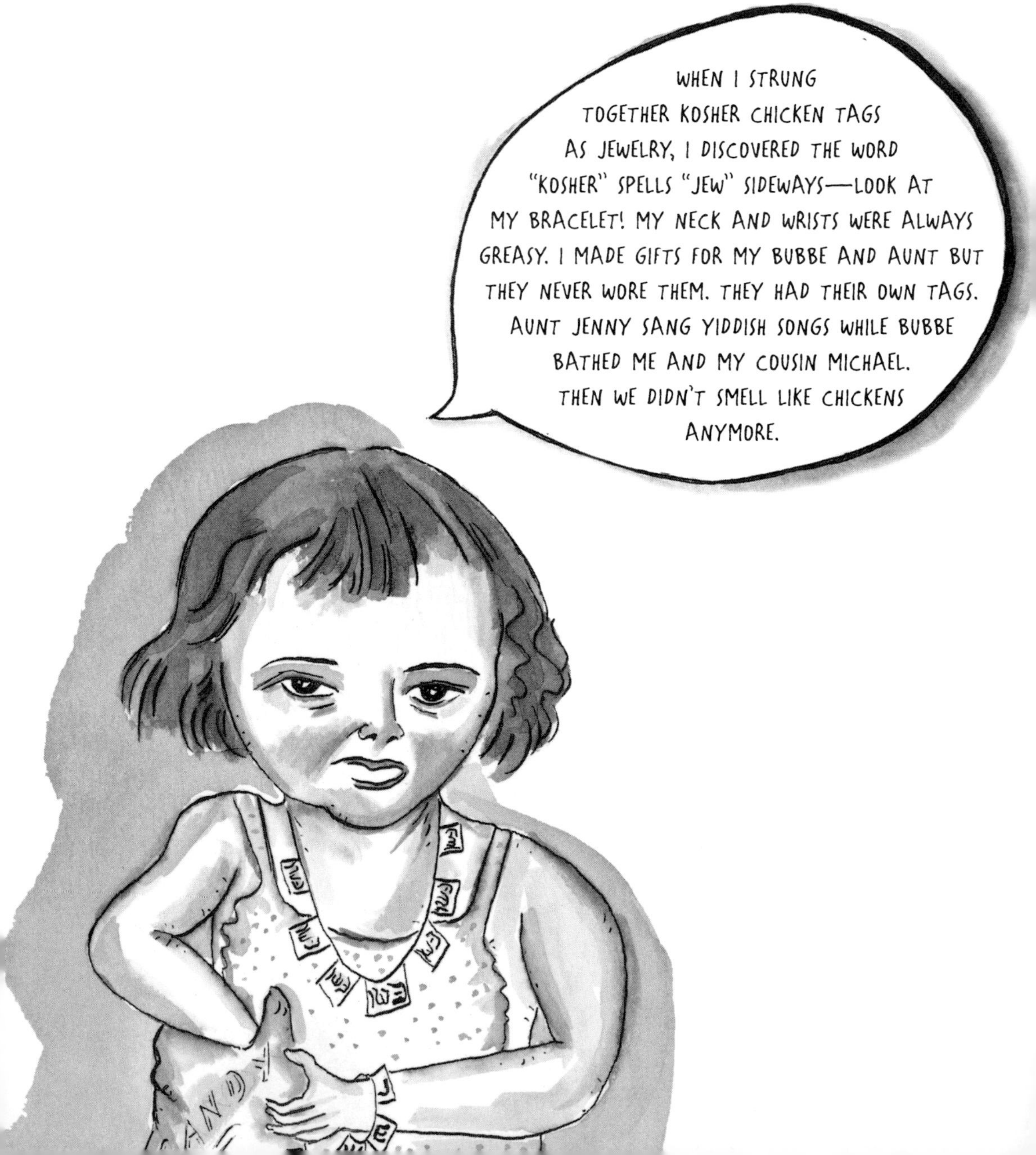
WHEN I STRUNG TOGETHER KOSHER CHICKEN TAGS AS JEWELRY, I DISCOVERED THE WORD "KOSHER" SPELLS "JEW" SIDEWAYS—LOOK AT MY BRACELET! MY NECK AND WRISTS WERE ALWAYS GREASY. I MADE GIFTS FOR MY BUBBE AND AUNT BUT THEY NEVER WORE THEM. THEY HAD THEIR OWN TAGS. AUNT JENNY SANG YIDDISH SONGS WHILE BUBBE BATHED ME AND MY COUSIN MICHAEL. THEN WE DIDN'T SMELL LIKE CHICKENS ANYMORE.

Yiddish Holds the World

Is it funny enough, is it sad enough? Am I too whiny,
too angry, too petulant? Boo hoo, poor little survivors'
child. Have I managed to avoid using every cliché there is
out there relating to the Holocaust? You see, I have this
problem—growing up in the household of my parents
was not tragic, but their past was. My life was not cursed,
theirs was. They were born under an unfavorable star
and forced to sew it onto their clothing. Yet here I am,
some Jewish Sisyphus, pushing history and memory
uphill, wondering what I'm supposed to be, and what I
really feel like is a rebellious child, wanting to stand
before my parents and say, Here, take it—it's yours,
I don't want it. But all I have to do is look up ahead and
catch a glimpse of Primo Levi and Elie Wiesel, Founding

Fathers of Memory, fixed at the very top, in order to realize my folly. Look what it has taken for them to find their words.

A tsigayner melody iz azoy sheyn A GYPSY MELODY IS SO BEAUTIFUL hert ir es, fargest ir es nit, neyn THAT ONCE YOU HEAR IT, YOU WILL NEVER FORGET IT

At the same time, I can't help myself from wondering: What did the floor around Primo Levi's desk look like? Was it littered with hundreds of wrinkled-up pieces of paper, ideas thrown out because he felt his words lacked, did not even come close to the truth of his

git es keyn ru, AND IT GIVES NO REST, s'farkisheft aykh di melody YOU'RE SPELLBOUND BY THE MELODY.

experience. Did Elie Wiesel feel the frustration of having to find new ways of saying the same thing over and over again, causing him to put his pen down and roll his eyes heavenward. Did he happen to have a thesaurus on the Holocaust as a guide, and every time, stymied, he could look up a word, say like "crematorium," and find just the right fresh noun. "See under oven: an enclosed compartment of brick, stone, or metal for cooking food; furnace; kiln." And then he would try out a sentence: Auschwitz's enclosed compartments made out of brick and stone for cooking Jewish flesh worked 24/7. The sentence is crossed out, deleted, another one begun . . .

vayl zi iz varem, hartsik, ful mit kheyn BECAUSE IT IS WARM, SOULFUL, FULL OF CHARM. A modne kraft, A STRANGE CRAFT, zi git aykh libe un oykh lebnshaft IT GIVES YOU LOVE AND ALSO A LUST FOR LIFE. Hert ir es nor eyn mol HEAR IT BUT ONCE

Did either one of these writers consider whether something they said or wrote might be in bad taste, or did they write jokes in private that they knew could never be uttered outside their studies? Like this one: Max and Abe are walking towards an enclosed compartment made out of brick and stone, and Max turns to Abe and says, "What do you get when you lubricate an auditorium with a million Jews? A creamatorium." A real knee-slapper. Thankfully, this would have been crumpled up and added to an ever-growing pile of rejects.

ISN'T SHE BEAUTIFUL, MY AUNT JENNY? YOU CAN'T TELL THAT SHE HAS ONLY ONE ARM. MAYBE THAT'S WHY MICHAEL IS HOLDING MINE. JENNY CAN SING. SHE WON A PRIZE ON THE TED MACK AMATEUR HOUR. THE PROGRAM THAT SELLS GERITOL, THE ELIXIR OF LIFE— "ARE YOU TIRED, LISTLESS, RUN-DOWN? TRY GERITOL!" TOO BAD IT DOESN'T WORK. MICHAEL GREW UP TO HAVE CROHN'S AND A COLOSTOMY, AND JENNY NEVER TIRED OF WORRY. BUT JUST LISTEN TO HER SING A LONG-FORGOTTEN YIDDISH SONG.

It's difficult enough to discover the right words for what is to be remembered, but even harder

when each word longs to shelter and sustain the memory of a generation aged and now dying.

I was born in October 1949, in an area of downtown Toronto called Kensington Market. Bordered by Spadina Avenue, one of the city's main north-south arteries, the streets to the west—Augusta, Kensington, Baldwin, Nassau, Oxford—held a maze of narrow alleys and densely packed-together houses. Eastern European Jewish immigrants arrived in the early twentieth century and made their first homes here. Residents quickly set up shop with bolted-down pushcarts in front of their houses from which they sold a variety of goods. Those who prospered over time left their frame houses and moved north, to other parts of the city. After the war, room was made for the next wave of immigrants and, with them, *shtetl* life became transplanted and took root.

The day of my birth that year happened to coincide with Yom Kippur. I don't know whether or not my mother fasted on the eve, but her Day of Atonement provided a new name for the Book of Life. I've never been quite sure if being born on this auspicious date meant that from then on I was off the hook for feeling guilt over any deed or thought or so riddled with it that I believed

The Guide for the Perplexed, written centuries before my arrival by the Jewish philosopher Maimonides, was intended for me. Whatever. A state of confusion seemed an appropriate place to start from, especially within the labyrinth of Kensington Market, which was home for the first four years of my life.

Kensington Market is my babysitter, while my father and mother are in their shop just around the corner, plucking feathers from chickens.

I'm standing in front of the Lottmans' bakery on Baldwin Street, a pint-sized version of the Michelin Man, unable to move in my quilted snowsuit. Silver-coated sugar ball bearings—the kind that decorate wedding cakes and break your teeth when you bite into them—roll around in my hand. Someone from the bakery must have given them to me, and anyway, the broken baby tooth of a child would not be such a tragedy.

The warm smell of baked goods escapes each time a customer goes in or comes out, and instead I wish I had been given a Nothing—a puffed baked confection sprinkled with sugar, manna from heaven. Who would have named something "nothing"? Probably the same person who first tasted the sweet and then, with a shrug, said in Yiddish, *"Vus eppes"*—literally, "What something." It should have been called a Something from the start, but that would have been too simple. *Vus eppes*, go figure. It must be itself and its opposite at the same time, both present and absent, much like this place from the past where I stand.

Across the street is the cheese emporium, displaying giant wheels of cheese in the window. From the market's small, narrow stores, all crowded one on top of the other, everything can be purchased. Fish fresh from a tank or scaled and filleted, chicken plucked and trussed or sectioned into parts, barrels of herring—brined and pickled—barrels of pickles—brined and pickle-pickled —bagels, braided breads, rye bread, with or without kimmel, black bread, with or without raisins, and a cornucopia spill of fruit, vegetables, and nuts. Shopkeepers wear long white aprons, which are stained with the colors of their wares by hands wiping off blood from freshly killed poultry, meat, and fish or the pigmented juice of overripe fruit. Chickens, trying to cheat fate, can be seen roaming the concrete sidewalks and streets that might as well have been made of the straw and mud of the past.

The Anshei Minsk Synagogue on St. Andrew, with its Russian-Romanesque architecture, watches over the streets half a century before its windows will be broken, its books burned, in 2002. But for now it is still able to pulse klezmer music into the air and over the rooftops

of the market, cadences of the Yiddish soul, another
kind of sweet Nothing. Marc Chagall must have floated
paint onto his canvases in Russia with these sounds on
his brush.

Our first home in Kensington Market is an apartment
on the second floor of a house on Wales Avenue. There
are two bedrooms, one for the four of us, the other for
a boarder, Mr. Pick, with whom we share the kitchen and
bathroom. He was alone and old and I would come to
think of him as Mr. Toothpick, wanting to complete his
name so that he more closely resembled how I saw him—
skinny and tall. Sometimes after my mother bathed me,
while I was being dried off and changed, our lodger
would appear with a Life Saver tied to the end of a string,
which he dangled over my head to lick.

We lived on Wales for less than two years. In 1950, my mother's parents, Moishe and Machele, and my aunt and uncle, Jenny and Jacob (whom we called Jack), and their son, Michael, arrived from Sweden, where they had found themselves after the war. Finally, they are all reunited, and from then, my parents, my grandparents, and my aunt and uncle will live within close proximity to one another, no matter how often moving house was entailed.

My father and his brother buy a building on Spadina Avenue that has a grocery store on the street level. Jack will run the store while my father continues to work in his shop nearby on Kensington Avenue in the market. My grandparents find a home for themselves just a few streets away. When our family and Jack's merge under one roof, filling the two floors above the store, Mr. Pick is invited to gather his few belongings and move into the room in the attic, and the taste of candy on a string will sweeten a new home.

The wallpaper of my bedroom has cowboys and Indians on it and I'm crying. I am in a crib and my sister, Sharon, three years older than I am, is next to me, lying on her cot. My father is here, leaning close to Sharon with a doll in his hands, and when he sees me crying as he is about to give the doll to her, he turns and gives it to me. Just as he bends towards me, and before he places the doll in my arms, cowboys and Indians surround him. This is the moment when I first begin to ally my father with westerns.

SO, SANTA, HERE'S WHAT
I WANT—A DREYDL THAT
PLAYS MUSIC WHEN IT SPINS.
HAVE MY PARENTS STOP ARGUING SO
MUCH.... SANTA, BRING THEM ALL BACK.
AND IF YOU CAN'T DO THAT, THEN MAKE
ONE SNOWFALL TURN INTO ASH.

*Yiddish was
the soul and substance
of the life in our home.*
A *veltele*, a world within a
world. Looking back, it is
embodied in the intense
gaze of my father and in the
resilience of my mother. It
is in the stern silence of my
mother's father and in the
endurance of his wife, and
in the close presence of my
aunt and uncle. It is
every bar mitzvah,
wedding, picnic, and
weekend gathering of
my parents' friends.
Yiddish is spending
the summer at Wasaga
Beach, where several cottages make
up a *shtetl* of Greenie families, and watching overweight,
overtanned sunbathers bend, knee-deep in the lake,

MERRy CHANUKAH
1953

abluting themselves with scooped handfuls of water and sighing, "Ah, what a *mechaieh*," what a pleasure.

Yiddish was our home. It was outrunning my mother to the bathroom and locking the door so that she couldn't *patsh* my *tochis* again, and it was the *shreklech* shrieking of my parents' anger. It was the dining-room table laden with memorial *yorzeit* candles on Yom Kippur, the day's serious meaning relived for the rest of the year when we drank juice out of the small glass containers that once held enough wax to burn for twenty-four hours. It was the toasted rye bread rubbed with *knobl*, garlic, that I had for breakfast before being sent off to kindergarten with a salami sandwich, thickly sliced, spread with *shmaltz*. Yiddish was the medicinal remedy my mother used when she hollowed out a potato and placed it over my throbbing, badly burned thumb. Five pounds of potatoes later and a sizable infected blister, she finally allowed a doctor to prescribe antibiotics.

I don't remember hearing English as a language until I went to school. As my parents' English vocabulary grew they attached these words to Yiddish, although at the time I was only aware of

YOU MEAN YOU UNDERSTOOD WHAT I WAS SAYING?

WHO KNEW SHE WAS ALWAYS LISTENING!

one harmonic language being spoken. From an early age, my ear became tuned to hear words voiced with a certain cadence and pitch. To this day, any time my mother and I have a conversation, I absorb what she says without any consciousness of her mixing in Yiddish words.

The primary residence of Yiddish in our home managed to affect my relationship to English after I began to go to school. Example: Imagine that you've gone on holiday, a stranger in a strange land. You're all dressed up—*fartrasket*—ready to go out for an evening of exploration. You get into your rented car and drive for a while until you run out of gas on the highway on a country road in the middle of who knows where—that's a *farshtinkener* (really lousy) situation. Then you realize that you have *fargessen* (forgotten) to take your cell phone with you, having left it in your *farkrimmt* (crowded) hotel room, and you start to feel the whole holiday is *farkuckt* (screwed up). In hindsight, the excursion was poorly planned and the fault is yours and now you feel *farblondjet* (not only lost, but way off track). Suddenly a swarm of wasps comes out of the *finster* (dark) and you are completely *farpotshket* (messed up)

OF COURSE. YOU WERE ALWAYS SPEAKING YIDDISH.

WHAT IS IT WITH ALL THE ALTES! DON'T THEY KNOW THEY CREATED THE AIR I BREATHE? THE CHUTZPAH NOT TO THINK IT MATTERED. BUT I'VE ONLY JUST BEGUN TO LET THEM KNOW.

from head to toe. All is *farfolen* (lost). The day is *fertig* (finished) and you lie down in a *farkrimmt, farshtinkener, farkuckt* ditch by the side of the road.

Farshtaist? Understand?

With its syllabic repetitions, Yiddish often rattled the way I heard English when it was being spoken. Now in order to experience the full flavor of my predicament, start to speak and then sneeze at the same time. Try it: far-fetched, far-flung, far be it, forspent, foreshadow, for shame, furnish (could be confused with *gornisht,* nothing), forlorn, forbidden, foreplay, furtive (often confused with *fertig*), and fermented—one of my favorites because it sounds as if it should really mean something that was intended to be, as in fate.

In the late 1950s, I used to watch a TV show called *The Millionaire.* Every week, Michael Anthony was handed a check to deliver to some deserving individual, changing a life forever in American-dream-come-true-land. The only things revealed about the magnanimous benefactor, at the beginning of each show, were his voiceover, the sight of his two hands, and his name: John Bears Fartipton.

Or, at least, that's what I heard. Only much later, during a conversation about TV trivia, was I corrected: John Beresford Tipton. Even so, my spliced-together interpretation made more sense, since to be *fartipt* means to be askew, off-centered, which this man had to be if he was handing out one million dollars weekly. But instead of being a *meshuggener,* a crazy person, perhaps he was a televised version of the ultimate do-gooder, a genuine *tzaddik,* someone who will magically do God's bidding and then vanish, since a deed done anonymously is deemed the worthiest. "Heaven will know and God will remember."

Yiddish defines the world that I came from. It was the language that was spoken for most of my childhood years. It was my parents' mother tongue, their *mamaloshen*, filling every step they had taken from one country to the next. Once, when I was very young and never again, I saw my father sweep up crumbs from the living-room floor, using the wing of a goose, a *fledervish*, as a dust broom. He then burnt the small pile of crumbs, the *chometz*, on a plate, symbolically ridding our home of the last remnants of cereals and grains, the final readying of the house for Passover. As my father crouched low over the small fire in the corner of the room, I felt the wonderment of a strange sight and sensed for the first time the way the past and a language are fastened together.

This is where the aleph bet begins.

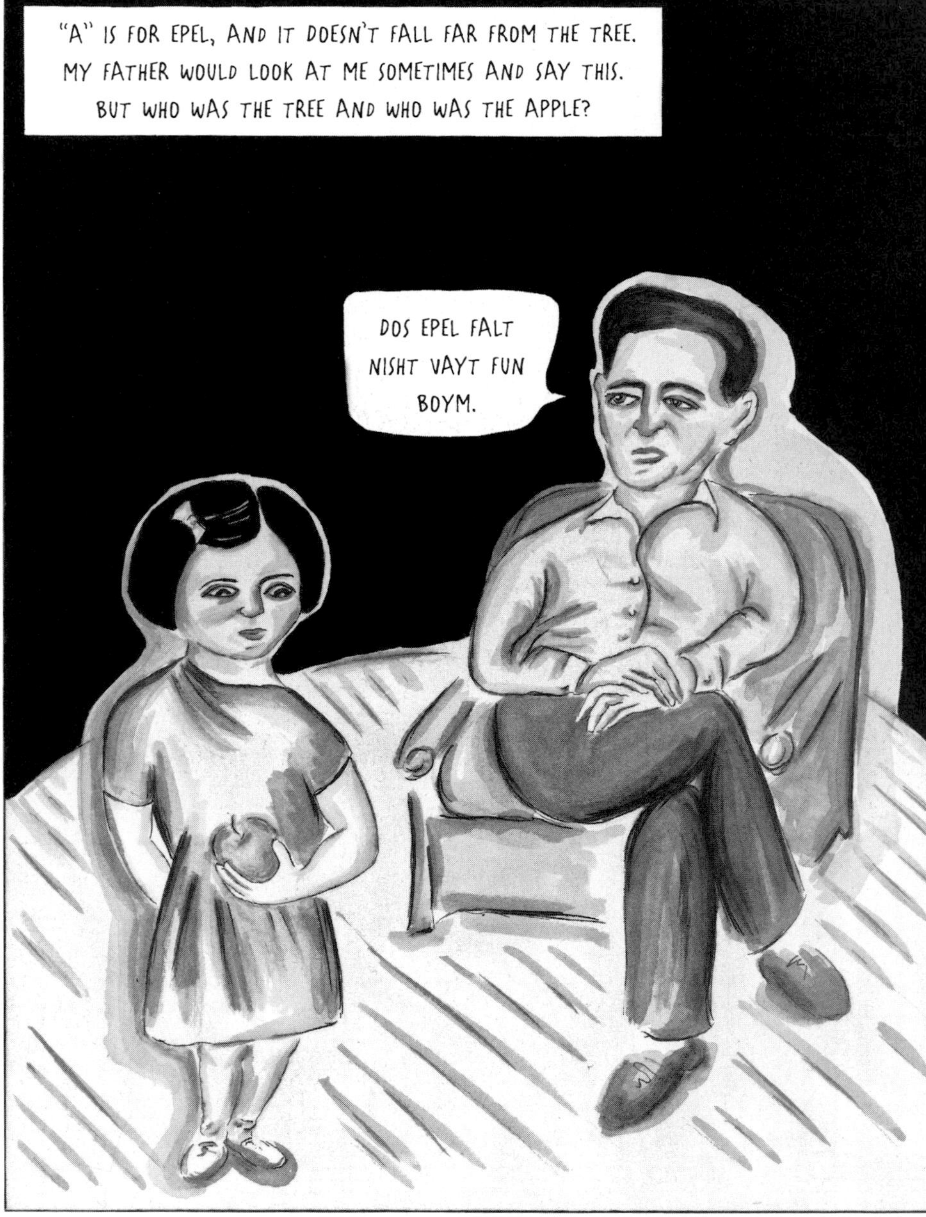
"A" IS FOR EPEL, AND IT DOESN'T FALL FAR FROM THE TREE. MY FATHER WOULD LOOK AT ME SOMETIMES AND SAY THIS. BUT WHO WAS THE TREE AND WHO WAS THE APPLE?
DOS EPEL FALT NISHT VAYT FUN BOYM.

DID IT FALL TO THE GROUND RIPE, OR AFTER A STRONG WIND TOOK THE FRUIT FROM ITS BRANCH?

EI! EI!

IS THAT AN EPPES I SEE BEFORE ME?

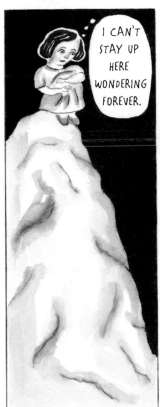

I CAN'T STAY UP HERE WONDERING FOREVER.

WHERE DO YOU LAND AFTER TAKING A LEAP OF FAITH? VUS EPPES— WHO KNOWS!

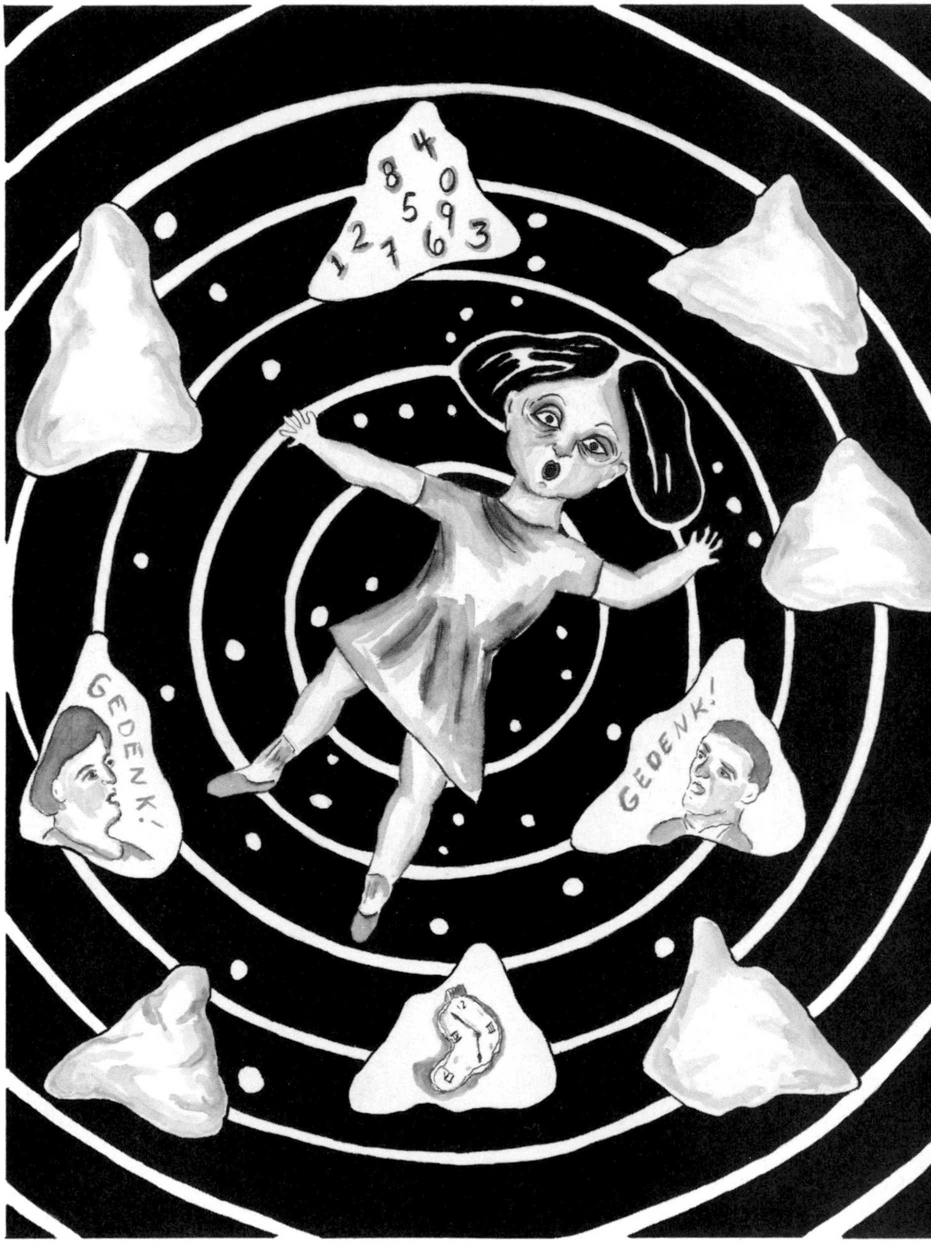
8 4
0
5
9
1 2
7
6
3
GEDENK!
GEDENK!

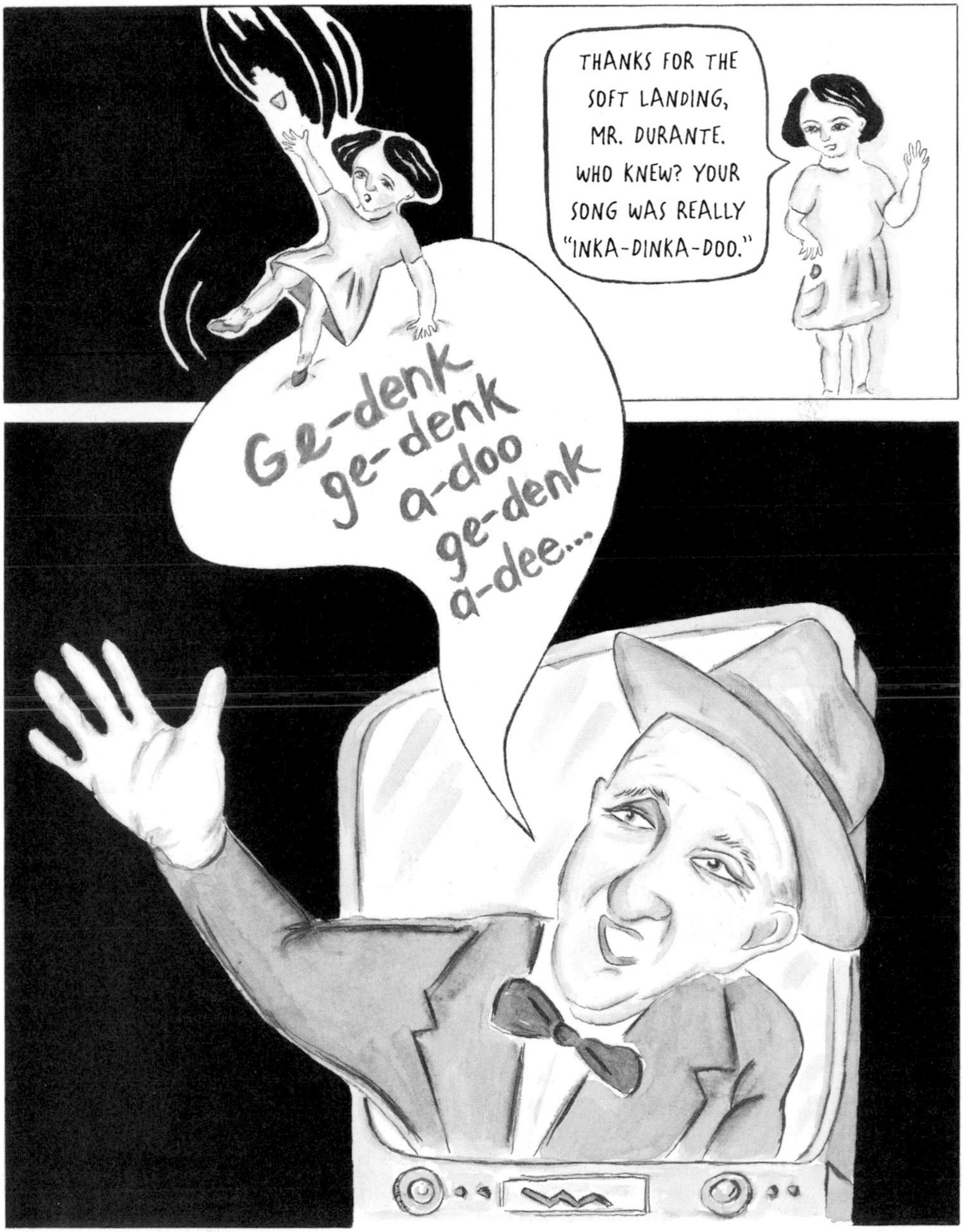
THANKS FOR THE SOFT LANDING, MR. DURANTE. WHO KNEW? YOUR SONG WAS REALLY "INKA-DINKA-DOO."
Ge-denk ge-denk a-doo a-denk ge-denk a-dee...

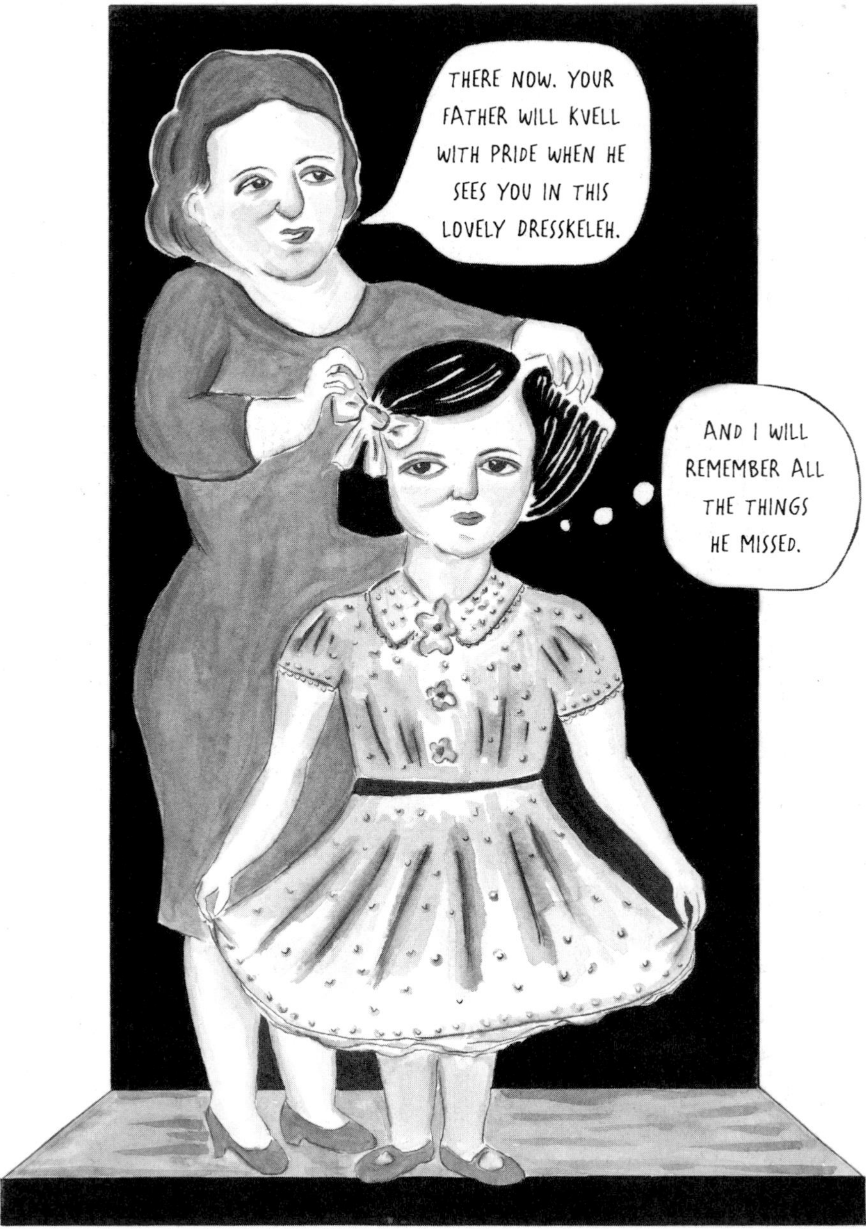
THERE NOW. YOUR FATHER WILL KVELL WITH PRIDE WHEN HE SEES YOU IN THIS LOVELY DRESSKELEH.
AND I WILL REMEMBER ALL THE THINGS HE MISSED.

ATTENDING HIS GRAND-
DAUGHTER'S BAT MITZVAH.

MORE DAYS—TO GROW OLD
WITH HIS WIFE.

MY PARENTS AND THEIR FRIENDS, ONCE THEY CAME TO A NEW LAND, NEVER KNEW THAT THEIR PAST DREW AN UNSEEN SHADOW OVER THE LIVES THEY BROUGHT INTO THE WORLD. ONLY THE SHADOW KNOWS AND IT IS TRYING TO SPEAK.

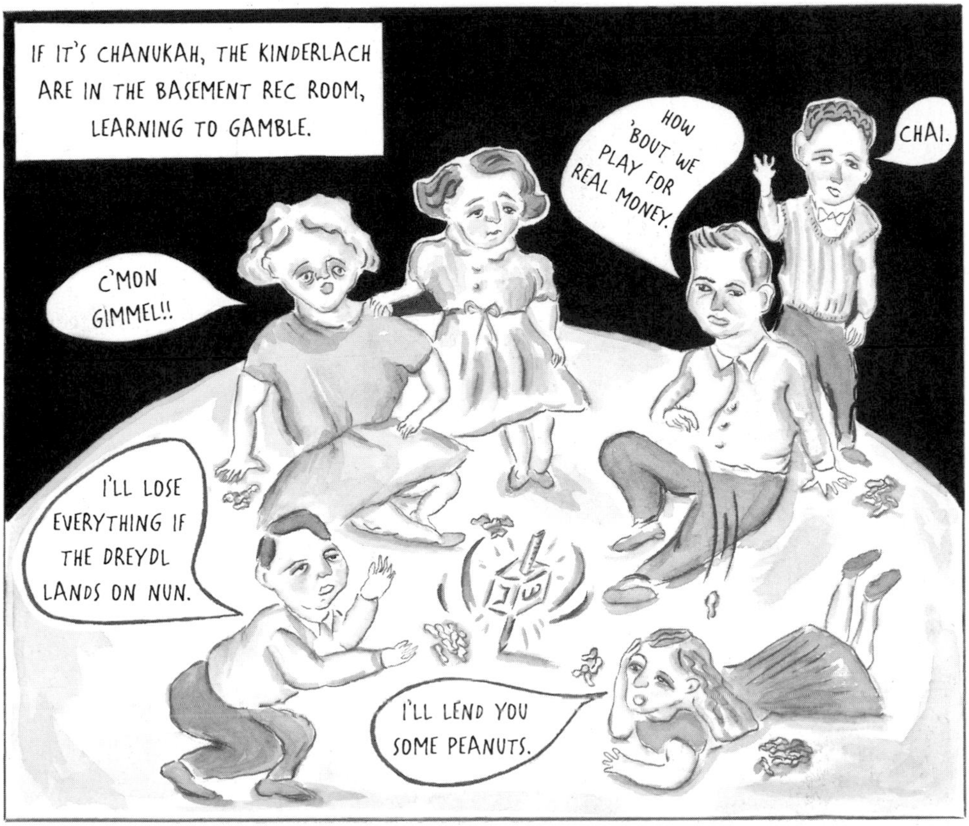
IF IT'S CHANUKAH, THE KINDERLACH ARE IN THE BASEMENT REC ROOM, LEARNING TO GAMBLE.
HOW 'BOUT WE PLAY FOR REAL MONEY.
CHAI.
C'MON GIMMEL!!
I'LL LOSE EVERYTHING IF THE DREYDL LANDS ON NUN.
I'LL LEND YOU SOME PEANUTS.

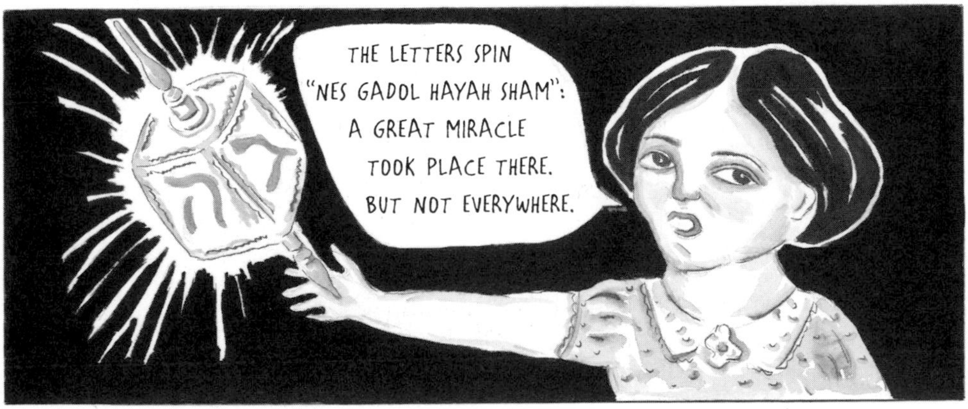
THE LETTERS SPIN "NES GADOL HAYAH SHAM": A GREAT MIRACLE TOOK PLACE THERE. BUT NOT EVERYWHERE.

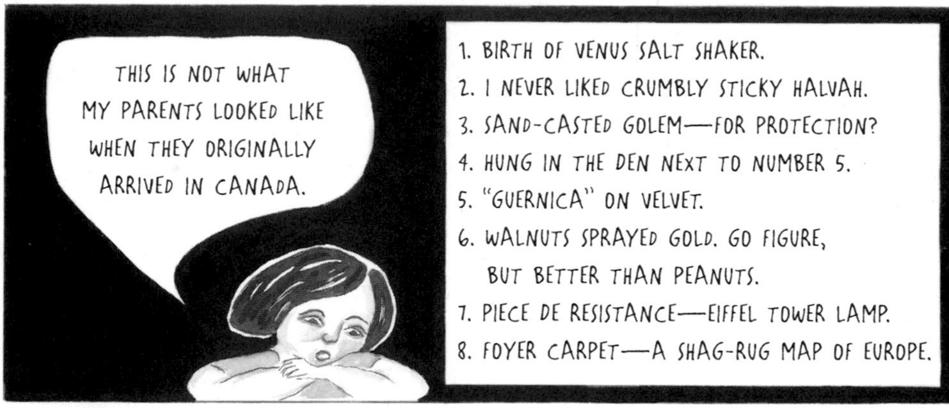
THIS IS NOT WHAT MY PARENTS LOOKED LIKE WHEN THEY ORIGINALLY ARRIVED IN CANADA.
1. BIRTH OF VENUS SALT SHAKER.
2. I NEVER LIKED CRUMBLY STICKY HALVAH.
3. SAND-CASTED GOLEM—FOR PROTECTION?
4. HUNG IN THE DEN NEXT TO NUMBER 5.
5. "GUERNICA" ON VELVET.
6. WALNUTS SPRAYED GOLD. GO FIGURE, BUT BETTER THAN PEANUTS.
7. PIECE DE RESISTANCE—EIFFEL TOWER LAMP.
8. FOYER CARPET—A SHAG-RUG MAP OF EUROPE.

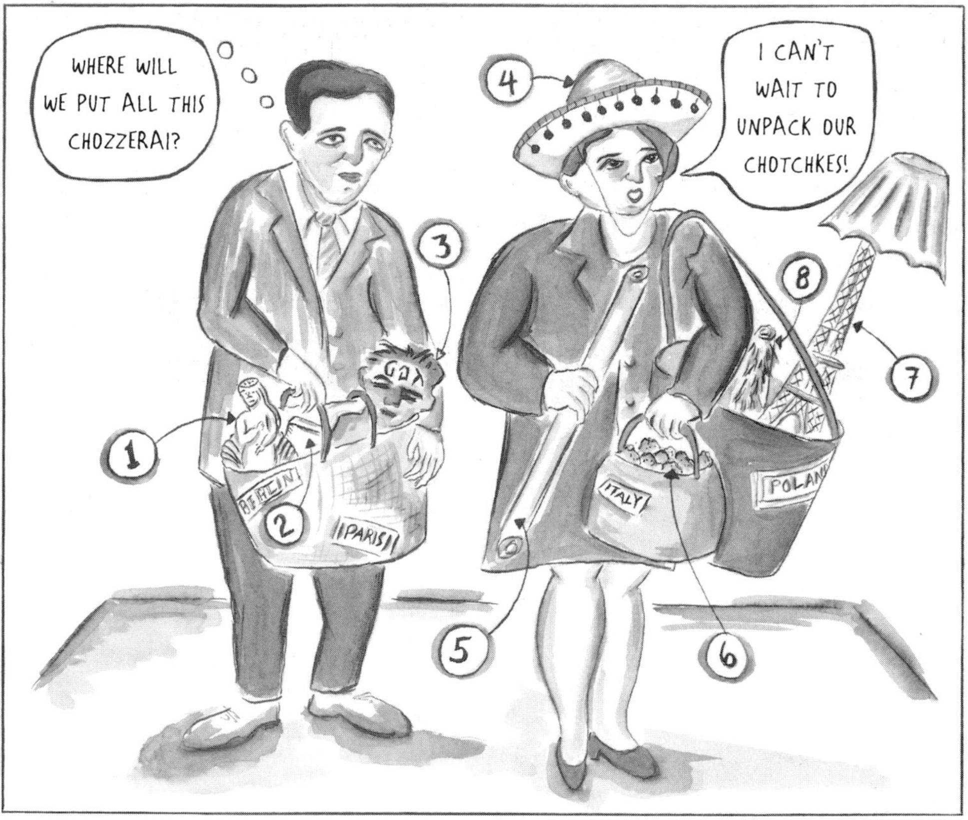
WHERE WILL WE PUT ALL THIS CHOZZERAI?
I CAN'T WAIT TO UNPACK OUR CHOTCHKES!
1
2
3
4
5
6
7
8
PARIS
ITALY
POLAN

CREAM CHEESE AND
LOX ON A BAGEL.
A BASHERT—THE ESSENCE
OF FATE, AND BELONGING
TOGETHER.

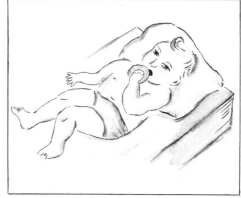

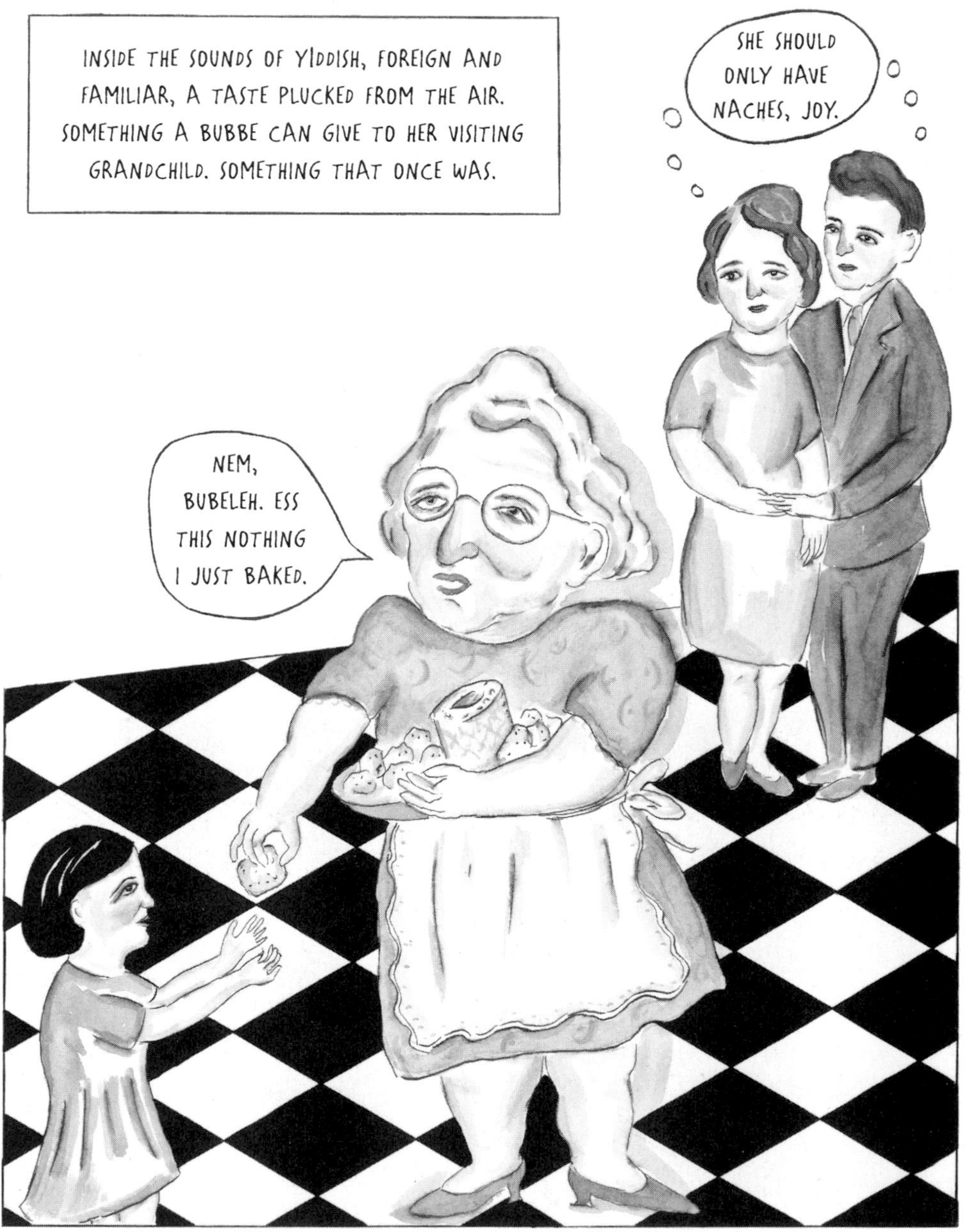
INSIDE THE SOUNDS OF YIDDISH, FOREIGN AND FAMILIAR, A TASTE PLUCKED FROM THE AIR. SOMETHING A BUBBE CAN GIVE TO HER VISITING GRANDCHILD. SOMETHING THAT ONCE WAS.
SHE SHOULD ONLY HAVE NACHES, JOY.
NEM, BUBELEH. ESS THIS NOTHING I JUST BAKED.

THERE'S A YIDDISH PROVERB:
IF WE ALL PULLED IN ONE
DIRECTION, THE WORLD
WOULD KEEL OVER. BUT
WHAT ABOUT CRUELTY?
DOES THE WORLD REALLY
NEED THIS IN ORDER
TO EXIST?

BETTER TO LISTEN TO
THE ONES WHO MAKE
YOU LAUGH OR
WONDER ABOUT SPACE
AND TIME THAN TO
THOSE WHO POISON
OUR DREAMS.

CONFUSED? A PHRASE HEARD AT A CELEBRATION AND ALSO WHEN OFFERING CONDOLENCE? OYF SIMCHAS— MAY WE MEET ON JOYFUL OCCASIONS.

A PHRASE TO ACKNOWLEDGE LOSS AND A WISH FOR A COMMUNITY TO GATHER NEXT AT BETTER TIMES.

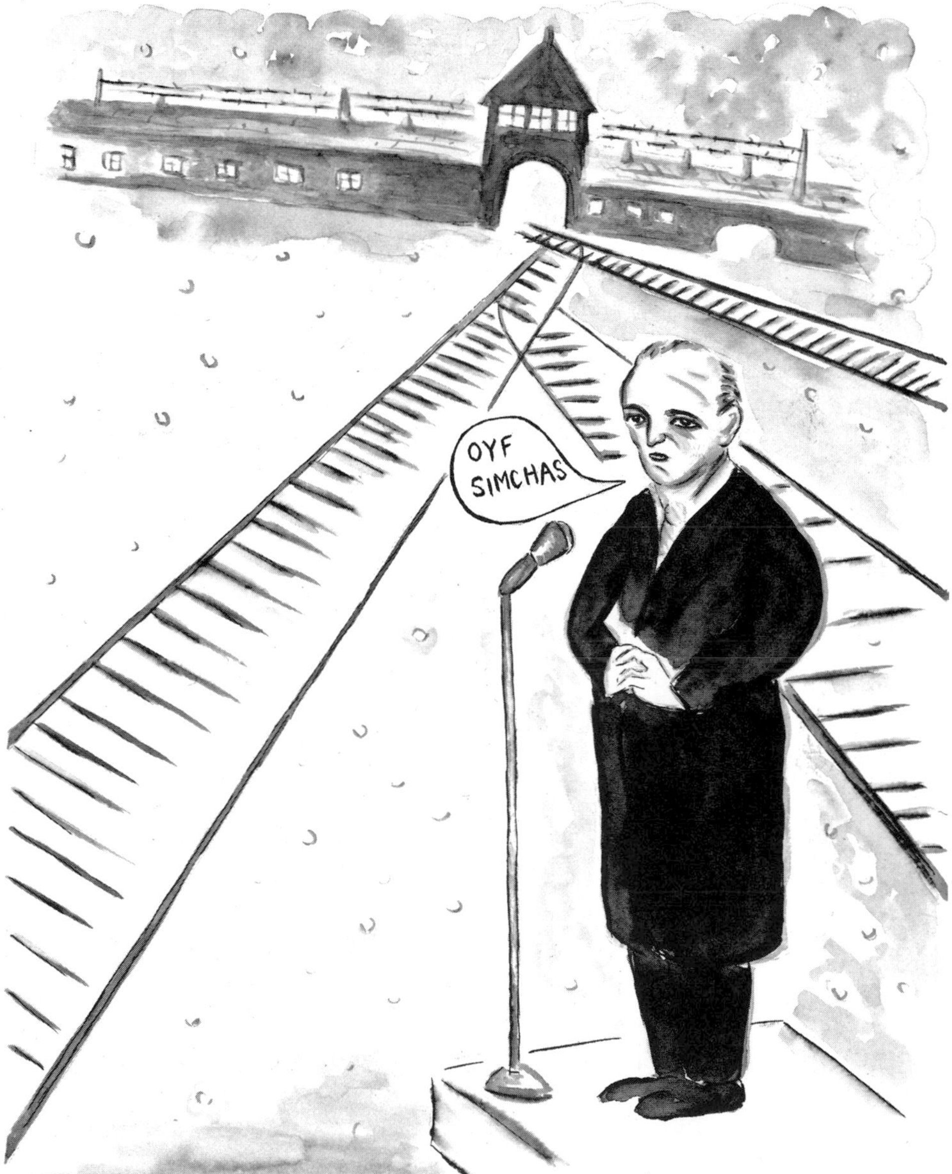
OYF SIMCHAS

I USED TO BE AFRAID OF THE DARK. SOMETIMES I'D TAKE A MEMORIAL CANDLE FROM HOME TO LEAD THE WAY.

OOPS, WRONG CAVE.

ALIENS LEFT EARTH WITH A SPECIMEN TO STUDY.

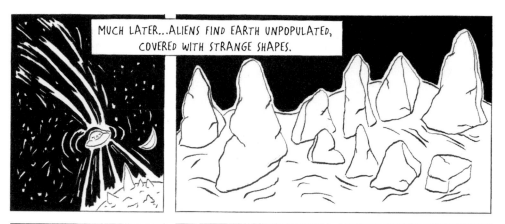

MUCH LATER...ALIENS FIND EARTH UNPOPULATED, COVERED WITH STRANGE SHAPES.

TRANSLATION: VUS EPPES!

THE LAST WANDERING JEW EXPLAINS THAT THE STONES ARE MEMORIALS. HE TELLS THE ALIENS TO CARVE THEM INTO NUMBERS. TEN VARIABLES THAT CAN BE ENDLESSLY COMPUTED, WITHOUT ANYONE LEFT TO DENY THEIR ACCURACY. AND IT WAS THE LAST TIME KADDISH WAS HEARD ON EARTH.

YISGADAL V'YISKADASH.

HOW CAN YOU DEAL WITH THIS KIND OF FARKUCKTEH LOGIC? THERE ARE OTHERS TO LEARN FROM, LIKE HANNAH ARENDT AND PRIMO LEVI.

ONE HUNDRED DEAD IS A CATASTROPHE. A MILLION DEAD— A STATISTIC.

THE MANIFESTATION OF THE WINDS OF THOUGHT IS NOT KNOWLEDGE; IT IS THE ABILITY TO TELL RIGHT FROM WRONG, BEAUTIFUL FROM UGLY.

IT'S NOT A MATTER OF ARRIVING AT THE DEEPEST ROOTS OF KNOWING, BUT JUST OF GOING DOWN FROM ONE LEVEL TO ANOTHER, UNDERSTANDING A LITTLE MORE THAN BEFORE.

There is no center
to be found in memory,
to be found in memory,
but each place
holds its heartbeat.

"A" is for epel, and it doesn't fall far from the tree. When I was born, along with my English name, I was given the Yiddish names of my father's two sisters, Binche and Chana. Once, years later, when my hair was braided and pinned low behind my head, my father told me that I resembled his older sister, Binche. I could not read his expression at the time, but as my father found his way back to his family through me, I felt that moment's tender fusing of pleasure and loss.

One day, a couple of years ago, my aunt Jenny received from a friend a copy of the memoir he had written about his experiences in the war. He was a *landsman*, a fellow countryman, from Miechow, my father's and uncle's hometown, and the family had kept in touch with him after the war when he settled in America. My aunt said that in a section of the book about the liquidation of the Miechow ghetto, there was information about Binche, and she went on to tell me what she had read. The only things I knew about Binche, from what my father had told me, were that she died in the war, that she had been pregnant, and that she had perished along with her parents, her sister, and her husband. If he knew more about her, he did not speak of it to me or, as I was to learn, to my mother.

A few days later, my mother received her own copy of this memoir and it was then that I read what this gentle man had witnessed and then written about in simple, unadorned language, leaving me without distance from what he had seen.

On Saturday morning, September 4, 1942, the remaining fifteen hundred Jews of Miechow were rounded up by German soldiers and marched out of the ghetto to the railroad station. There were already hundreds of people there, gathered from the surrounding area. People were crying, and children, lost, were screaming for their mothers. My father's parents were there, along with his two sisters, Binche now pregnant, and Binche's husband, Mintz, whom she had married a year earlier in the ghetto.

Binche went into early labor with a group of women surrounding her, trying to help deliver her baby. The sound of her cries were deep and painful, and for a long time, her witness wrote, they entered his sleep. Binche's child was born and then immediately shot.

Because the man's brief account of my father's sister ends here, we will never know for certain whether Binche was killed right after or forced onto the train with the others, with her husband, her sister, her parents, and taken to Treblinka in eastern Poland. The words of Kaddish, the mourner's prayer, were not recited, but now the testimony of a man unknown to me has brought back her name, completing my own, allowing me to place a stone on an unmarked grave.

Later, I ask my mother about this gentleman, who had not been part of the transport that day because he was among a group of a hundred young men who had been selected to be sent elsewhere to work. Her own past stirs and she begins to speak about the time just after Liberation when she and my father lived in an apartment in the town of Katowice, where they were married. She tells me that this man had been a friend of my father's, from his home, and that he had been a tailor. After the war, he'd come through Katowice, and having learned that my father was there, ended up staying with them for a few days before going on.

I wonder, as my mother speaks, whether this man who knew my father and his family had ever told my father what he had witnessed. I have to ask one more question, wanting to know if my father had been spared from what we now have to remember. When I do, my mother assures me that my father, whom she knew so deeply, had never been told what happened to his sister that day.

With her answer, time falls away and I see two survivors embrace, welcoming each other back to life, with their nightmares privately held, entrusted to memory alone.

A is for *aleha ha-sholem*. On her, peace. Spoken for Binche, for my father's sister.

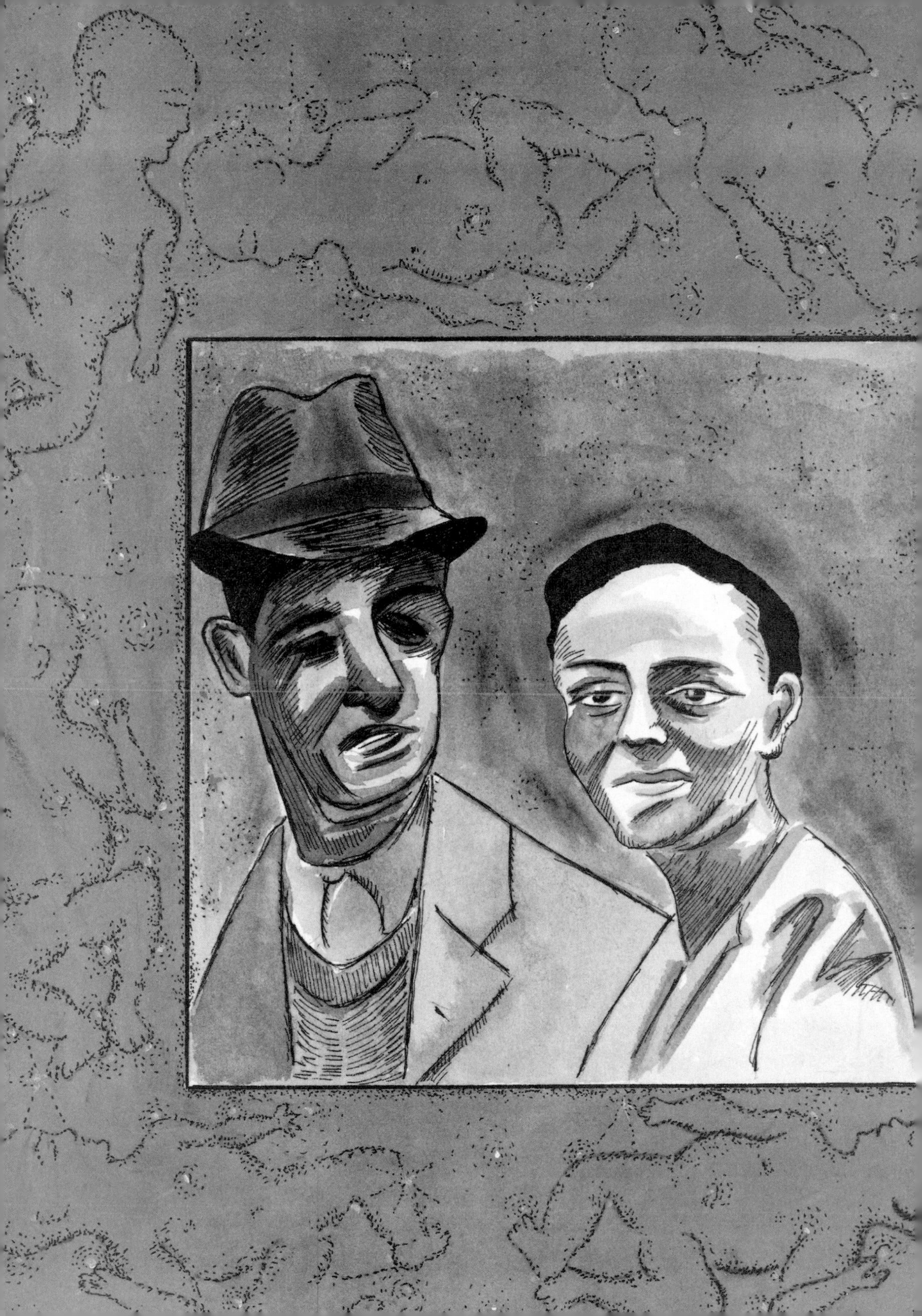

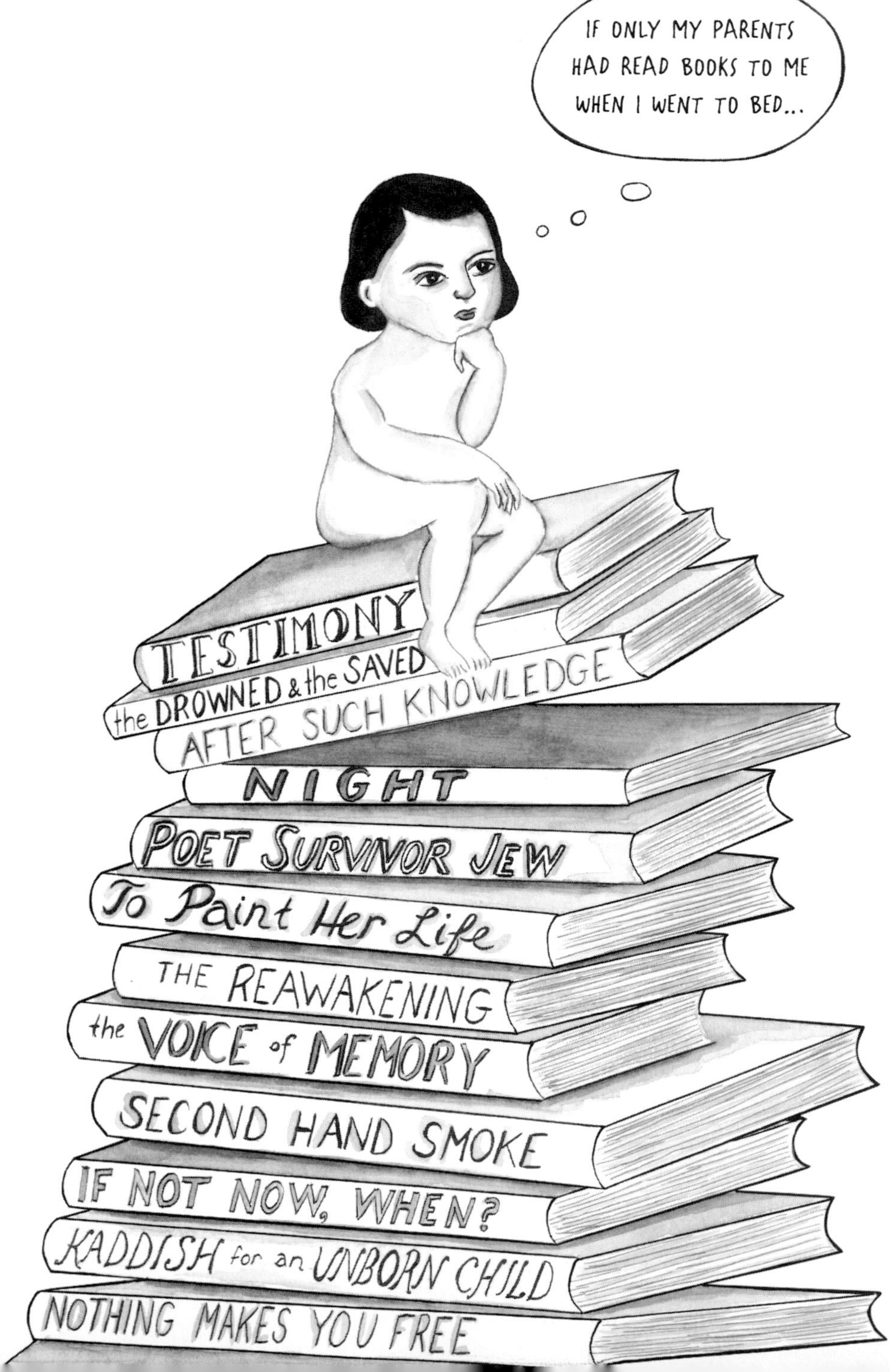
IF ONLY MY PARENTS HAD READ BOOKS TO ME WHEN I WENT TO BED...
TESTIMONY
the DROWNED & the SAVED
AFTER SUCH KNOWLEDGE
NIGHT
POET SURVIVOR JEW
To Paint Her Life
THE REAWAKENING
the VOICE of MEMORY
SECOND HAND SMOKE
IF NOT NOW, WHEN?
KADDISH for an UNBORN CHILD
NOTHING MAKES YOU FREE

The Meaning of Books

There were no books or paintings lining the rooms in the
home where I grew up. My parents read the newspaper,
keeping themselves in step with the events of the day. The
only concerts we ever attended were on Sunday mornings
when *The Yiddish Hour* filtered into the kitchen as we ate
our breakfast. On those days, there would be a *mish-mosh*,
a cacophony of sounds, stacked one on top of the other.
"Barek, get up, breakfast is on the table." Sounds of
splashing from the bathroom, the clatter of dishes,
my mother's intentionally heavy footsteps, making sure
everyone in the household was awake. Music pouring out
of the radio, with the Andrews Sisters singing "Bei Mir
Bist Du Schon."

I SAW LUST FOR LIFE AND FELL IN LOVE WITH ALL
COLORS. THIS IS WHEN I FIRST BEGAN TO DRAW.

Though every room of the house was filled with my
parents' world, it was only natural that I would be drawn
outside by what was beyond our door. While growing up,
and not on schooldays, going out that door on Saturdays
was easy since my parents worked on that day too, leaving
my sister and me in each other's care. Once my brother,
Michael, was born, we often looked after him, happy to
have a life-sized doll to change and dress up.

If, over the years, I had the sense of benign parental
neglect, eventually I saw it differently. The circumstances

of my parents' lives had taught them to guard their stories, even after arriving in Canada when the sanction of safety restored their spirit. They must have believed that the country that took them in after the war would also carefully shepherd their children. And while I was too young to understand that I had already been shaped by the shadow of my parents' past, I was also unaware that once outside I would discover my own.

The Vaughan cinema on St. Clair Avenue was just a few blocks away from our new house on Braemore Gardens, a circular street north of downtown. When I was very young, my mother had taken me to see a movie there. It was *Oklahoma!* The women were dressed in gingham and the men floated on horses through a sea of corn, everyone singing and dancing the whole time, and when poor Judd died and the music became slow and heavy, I hid under my seat, frightened but enthralled. And thus began a love affair in the dark that has lasted throughout my life and will continue until my own credits run out.

BRIDGE ON THE RIVER KWAI TAUGHT ME THAT WHISTLING DOESN'T PREVENT EVERY DISASTER.

AFTER I SAW SOMETHING OF VALUE, A FILM ABOUT THE MAU MAU UPRISING, I CHECKED UNDER MY BED AT NIGHT TO MAKE SURE BAMBOO STAKES WEREN'T WAITING TO GROW THROUGH MY SLEEPING BODY.

The first time I went to the movies alone I was six years old and it was a Saturday. I would quickly come to learn that a search underneath the couch pillows miraculously provided enough for a ticket each time, and if there were a few extra coins, I could buy a bag of popcorn. From the start, the world of Technicolor awakened my dream to become an artist, and over time my head filled with romance, adventure, and drama as I took in stories about love lost and regained, about heroism in a jungle or a classroom, about the dedicated spirit of doctors, scientists, and explorers. But then the Holocaust arrived in Hollywood and the new images I saw, stripped of color, penetrated deeper and were filled with something different yet strangely familiar, connecting to my parents' past, darkening its shadow and adding resolution to mine.

THE PAWNBROKER CONFIRMED THAT THE PHYSICAL PAIN YOU CAN INFLICT UPON YOURSELF IS NOTHING COMPARED TO THE WEIGHT OF THE GHOSTS YOU CARRY.

I was eight years old when I saw *The Diary of Anne Frank* and I stopped playing hide and seek with the kids on the street and started looking for goodness in people. Afterwards, I asked my sister to show me how to draw a swastika. As we lay on the floor of our bedroom, covering sheets of paper with heavy black lines, I feared that while creating this evil image we were entering forbidden territory and might unleash a hideous power we could neither comprehend nor control. But nothing happened, and though we didn't say a word to each other, I knew that my sister and I both shared the same thought: Shh—don't tell Mommy and Daddy.

THE THREE FACES OF EVE MADE ME THINK VAN GOGH'S MOOD SWINGS WERE REASONABLE.

Einstein observed that the only reason for time is so that everything doesn't happen at once. But I can well imagine that he scratched his head, perplexed or bemused, when in 1905 his Special Theory of Relativity made its debut along with the infamous book proclaiming a Jewish world conspiracy, *The Protocols of the Elders of Zion*. In the year that science took its biggest leap forward in the understanding of mass and energy, the masses used their energy to blame everything on the Jews. Fifty years later, when I turned five, my own universe expanded when, in continual molecular motion, the alphabet reconfigured itself into comprehension—*Eureka!*—and I learned to read. At the same moment, the infinite possibility of Einstein reached zero and he died.

I remember the excitement of playing with letters, moving them about and uncovering new words. It was a game I had learned at school. With each step, one letter from a word was removed and then replaced with another: tame, time, tome, tomb. *A* is for *aktion, anschluss. A* is for absolution. Blank became black; crave, carve; laughter, slaughter; falter, alter; ember, remember. Words became clues to follow and codes to decipher, and I couldn't help but wonder if there had been others, in the past, who had played as I did. Command, kommandant, commandment; cast, outcast; vision, revision; Torah, torch; smote, smoke; gash, gas, ash.

Once I began to read, I could follow the unending trail left by writers, in order to try to understand what I could not comprehend.

The sense of companionship that I first felt when I held a book in my hands, before even opening it, has never left me. I read voraciously, anything and everything, and shortly after one book was closed I'd pick up another. I followed Beatrix Potter to A. A. Milne to J. D. Salinger; Harold Robbins to Hemingway to Dostoevsky; Anne Frank to John Steinbeck and Proust; Leon Uris to Isaac Bashevis Singer, Gertrude Stein, and Kafka, ad infinitum. I had entered into the private company of strangers and have listened ever

since to where they have taken me. Their thoughts lead me to discover other meanings in my own.

I have always been moved when one book speaks to another, expanding what I had first understood. I read a book called *The Voice of Memory*, a selection of thirty-six of

Primo Levi's interviews given between 1961 and 1987. In 1984, when Levi was asked how he was able to write *If This Is a Man*, one of his best-known books about his survival in Auschwitz, he said that writing it worked for him "as a sort of 'prosthesis,' an external memory set up like a barrier between my life today and my life then." It is the only time that "prosthesis" appears in the book, and the word lingers . . .

Philip Roth's unflinching gaze at humanity and the brilliance of his words and ideas make him one of the great writers. Some time later, after reading Levi's book, I read *The Plot Against America*, Roth's fictionalized conjecture about what would have happened if America had elected an anti-Semitic president during the Second World War, and I was once again full of awe. The novel, which opens in 1940, is narrated by a boy named Philip Roth. The writer has imagined himself as a child in a country infected with fear and hatred of the Jews, a hatred that has ignited hysteria. On the final page of the novel, after a neighboring boy's mother has been killed in a pogrom and is taken into Philip's household, I see the word again. "The boy himself was the stump, and until he was taken to live with his mother's married sister in Brooklyn ten months later, I was the prosthesis."

I know that Roth knew Levi's work, and undoubtedly had great respect for it. Roth had interviewed Levi at his home in Turin, Italy, and their conversation was published as an afterword to the 1996 edition of *Survival in Auschwitz*. Was Roth's use of the word "prosthesis" an unconscious reference to Levi all those years later, or was the echo his private call and homage to the memory of this profoundly important writer? To all that Levi experienced and remembered, to the responsibility of memory.

I read books to hear those whose voices have been silenced or lost, to discover what I have not been told. Once, I showed my father *The Book of Alfred Kantor*, wanting to bring him something that had impressed me so much. The book was of Kantor's own drawings, many of which were accompanied by hand-written descriptions. During the war, Kantor had been imprisoned in three concentration camps: Terezin, Auschwitz, and Schwarzheide. He was a young artist when the war began, and he sketched what he saw and experienced. Some of those drawings survived but most were lost or destroyed. After Liberation, while in a DP camp in Deggendorf, he recreated his testament and made drawings from memory. The book was published twenty-five years later. When I first looked through Kantor's visual recounting of what he had gone through, I experienced the despair in a man's life in a way that was different from anything I had taken in before from what I'd read or seen. The images were much more than drawn documentation, they were visceral memory exposed.

I had never shared a book with my father but I was hoping this one might be of interest to him and that we could talk together about it. When I presented it to him, he turned a few pages only, looking briefly at the drawings

there, and then he closed the book. "*Ich kenish* . . .
I can't look at this." He got up and walked out of the
room, leaving me upset with myself that I hadn't better
anticipated his reaction, and feeling sick with regret that
I had opened up his pain.

In the quiet of the kitchen, I realized that I had needed
my father to recognize the importance this book held for
me, but once again that sorrowful time in his life pulled
itself back out of reach, severing a connection between
us. Later, I saw for the first time how similar we were.
He could not speak about the past, and because I was
unable to trace my way there, it was difficult for me to
reach my own feelings. That day, my father and I were
both without the means to say what was in our hearts.

I buy books for many reasons. I sometimes
buy them for their covers. A drawing or a photograph
can stop my eyes from glancing farther over the book-
store's piled array. I will pick up the book and turn to
the dedication page and read the author's recording
of names, penned in gratitude and acknowledgment,
with devotion, with love, in memoriam, and I feel
the invitation into an intimate realm.

I read to become all-feeling as the daughter of parents
who have experienced unimaginable loss. I read in order
to be brave, to learn how to navigate my way through a
shape-shifting world. I read for the pure pleasure of how
language serves both imagination and will, and to hear
the clarity of voices responding to murky reality. In doing
so, I discover time and again the ability to find my own.

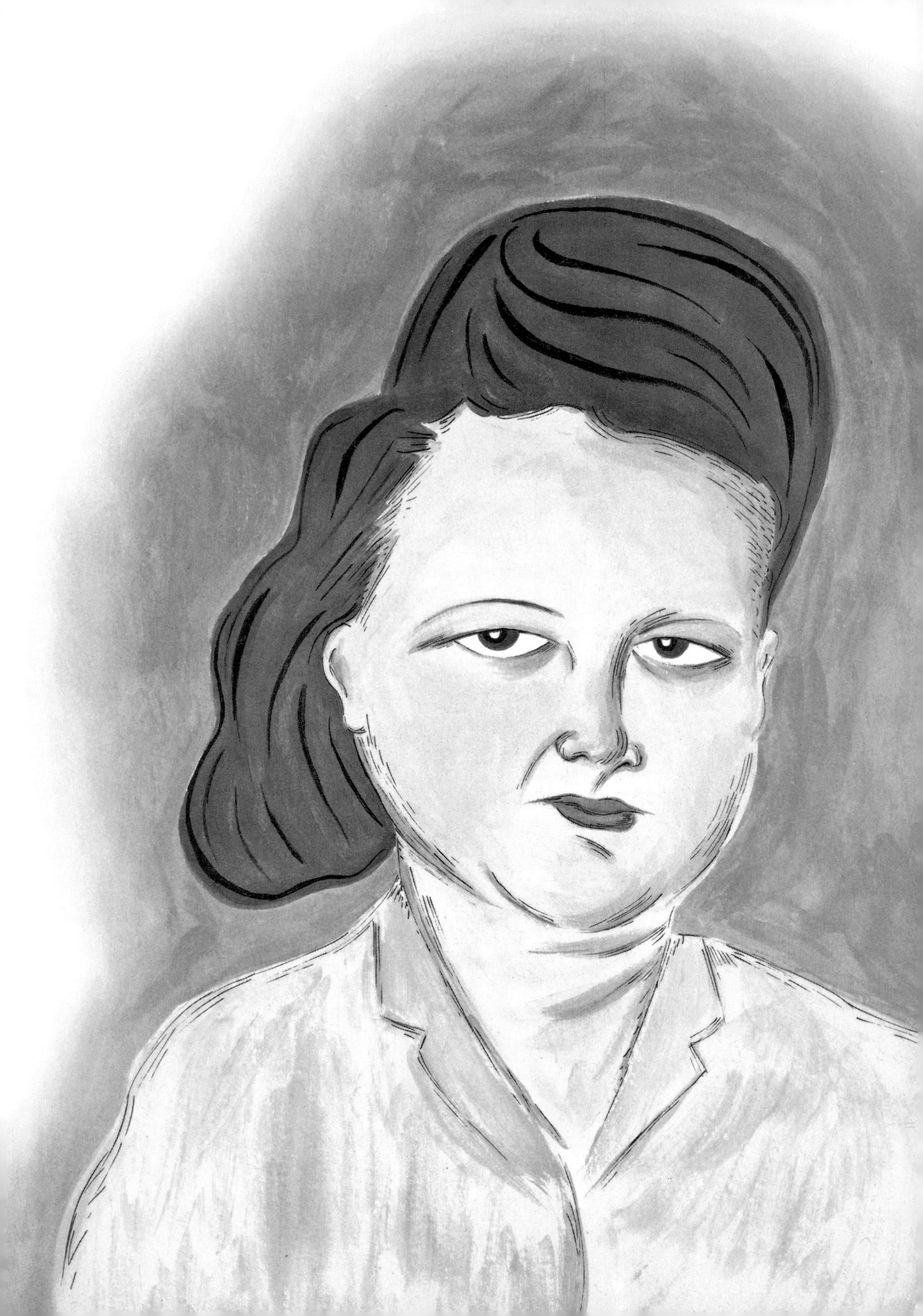

My Mother on Tape

When I was young, my mother and I used to walk together
and she'd hold my hand, her first steps setting the pace,
like a conductor measuring the beat. She always looked
straight ahead while I stared at the ground, drawn to
the motion of our feet. Perhaps memory is at its
most earthbound when I think of my mother.
Today we are on our way to visit Mr. Pick.
I'm six years old, and I haven't seen him since
we moved into our Braemore Gardens
house, having left Spadina Avenue two
years ago. My mother has told me that
he asked to see me, and the room we
now enter is in a hospital. She leads
me to his bed and delivers my hand

into his, then sits down on a chair. I can't recall whether Mr. Pick was awake or if he saw me, but I sensed that the quiet of the room and his body wrapped white with a sheet were somehow the same. I don't think that our visit lasted for very long and soon my mother and I are back on the street, our syncopated steps falling into the natural rhythm of the day.

My mother didn't tell me that Mr. Pick was dying, yet I felt the importance and seriousness of the moment. There had been a simple promise to fulfill. In her escorting me to see him, I sensed my mother and I had both become part of honoring a dying man's request. The gentle presence of this kind man, who had been a boarder with our family, had been acknowledged.

It wouldn't be hard for me to picture my mother just before we left our home that day when the usual routine was altered. She would have already finished preparing that evening's meal, the kitchen left clean and the house tidied. She would have brushed my hair, making sure that I was neat, and then she would attend to herself. She'd apply fresh lipstick, put on the beaded sweater she had made, then take my hand, and we'd set out. This same clear sense of purpose and practical outlook were what enabled my mother, many years later, to sit in a chair and speak directly to a camera for two hours.

In 1995, my mother agreed to be taped while answering questions posed by an interviewer, for the Archives of the Holocaust Project, which had been initiated by Steven Spielberg's Shoah Foundation. Later, she gave me a copy of the video, a tape that I watched, and watched again in order to be able to write my mother's story as she told it.

She sat before me, poised in a chair, and when I heard the precision and directness of her words I was transfixed. She spoke only in English, something I rarely heard my mother do, in the same unfaltering voice of someone who has chosen to speak, a voice I recognized from other documentaries I had seen. There was something in her controlled objectivity that initially caused me to feel distanced, but as I listened to my mother, I discovered the courage she has always possessed. Her story, which she had told me only in pieces when I was growing up, was now sequenced as best her memory would allow. I watched her set the pace with a steady bearing and, with her, I was able to look straight ahead.

I am Regina Eisenstein. Oksenhendler was my maiden name. I was born in 1925, in Bedzin, Poland, in the Zaglembia region, not far from the German border. Just before I turned fourteen, in 1939, war broke out. Bedzin was an industrial town, with thirty thousand Jewish families. I have a sister, Jadzia [Jenny], two years younger, and a brother, Lemel, three years younger. On September 4, when the Germans came, there was panic. The synagogue in the center of the city burned, Jews were chased out of their homes, and people were shot on the spot. Many had their houses burned down. There were roundups for unknown reasons. Jews were accused of atrocities and punished. Food was cut off and black-marketing was begun. Engagement in this activity became another excuse for the Germans' unjust arrests. Non-Jewish neighbors avoided Jews in the first few months. At this point, there was no formalized ghetto. The Judenrat was formed, a committee for the Jews to be organized. Food was rationed and a curfew was in place. In the evening, shots were heard, and the next morning we would find out whose house had been raided and who had been killed.

A Jewish police was established; some were hostile, some did the job right. Businesses were taken over by German officials, and Jews were given permits to be allowed to work. I worked making uniforms for German soldiers. This meant I had a working permit.

Always, different laws were created: Jews were not allowed jewelry, furs, cameras, household items. Any excuse to take away belongings, to murder someone.

There was a man who had engaged in black-marketing, he was trying to get food to sell to the community. He was caught and publicly hanged. I witnessed the hanging. I knew this man—he had tutored me and my brother and sister.

In 1940, there was a roundup, and my father, Moishe, was taken to Magstadt, in Germany, where he was to do roadwork, building a highway. News was smuggled out and we learned that he did not have enough food to eat and was beaten often while working.

Still there was no official ghetto in the town [the ghetto was established July of 1940], but slowly families from outside were forced to the center and moved together.

I had two good friends who were taken to concentration camps and I received mail from them. Their letters were sad and dreamy; they were lonely, heartbroken, hoping the war would end soon. Would we ever see one another? They both died. Later, someone had gone through a garbage dump from this camp, and the signed pictures I had sent to my friends had been found.

In the spring of 1940, there was another roundup, with the SS and dogs, and all the Jews were chased from their homes, ordered to a football field. We stayed there for two nights and days, in the rain and without food. We had to sit and wait. It was a terrible sight. Then we received news that a selection was to be made. The Jews were driven to the railway station, and the elderly and children with their mothers were sent off in boxcars. My grandparents were taken.

At this point, most families had been removed, families broken up. My aunts had been taken, and three cousins came to live with us, so now there were seven of us living together. Times were harder. We were afraid to even contact black-marketers for food. After the selection, there were rumors that the people had been taken to Auschwitz. It was hard to believe.

[The interviewer asks Regina if there was talk of escape amongst the Jews.]

It was only by the young. Money was needed for escape, for false identification papers. Harry Blumenfeld escaped. Then it was discovered that he had been arrested and taken to Auschwitz, where he was interrogated and killed.

In town, there were more selections. Those who had working permits had a better chance—they might not be picked. I was the only one in my family who had one, so I told my family to hide. When the SS came, I stood outside our door and said I was alone, that my family had gone.

After, I was overcome by the panic I felt and was hysterical. I knew there was worse to come. I felt like I'm dying.

Then the remaining Jews were ordered to move to the outskirts of Bedzin. We got one room with a foyer, for seven people. My mother, sister, brother, and three cousins.

REGINA'S AUNT, SARAH OKSENHENDLER, WAS A TEACHER AT THE BEDZIN ORPHANAGE, LOCATED AT THE EDGE OF THE CITY. IN 1943, THE ORPHANAGE WAS USED TO HOLD JEWS BEFORE DEPORTATION. CHILDREN WERE KILLED. SOME WERE SEEN BEING THROWN OUT OF THE WINDOWS.

We decided to build a hiding place. Behind the stove, we were able to dig out a partition, four feet by three feet, which would be hidden by a curtain above the stove. Also, under the bed, since there was a dirt floor, we made a small place to hide.

In August 1943, the ghetto was closed. At midnight, the SS and their dogs could be heard. There was gunfire. We hid. I went under the bed, and the others hid in the wall. The SS entered our home and thought the family had left to the gathering point, which was one mile away. At nightfall, I crawled out and looked through the window and saw that the ghetto is deserted, clothing scattered on the ground. There is no water from the taps. All we had to eat were some potatoes and oatmeal. My mother told us to drink our urine, but the three children said it did not taste good. We hid for a few days. It was unbearable. We were starving, and decided to go out from our home. My mother said we should try to clean ourselves up. When I looked in the mirror, I looked insane, not normal. An SS guard found us as soon as we walked out and took us to the sports field, where there were other remaining Jews. We were assembled and forced to march to the railway station. Poles looked the other way, smirking, as we passed. There were no signs of hope.

It took four to five hours to Auschwitz. People died. Once we had arrived, we came out of the boxcars, then were shoved onto the ramps, but at least there was fresh air.

Women and children and the old were sent away in dump trucks. I saw children taken from their mothers' hands; women begging to stay with their children were beaten and forced onto the trucks. As me and my family approached the selection, my brother Lemel tried to push himself among the men, seeing that would be better for him, knowing it was not good to be sent on the truck. Then we see that Lemel is on the truck, so quick, so chaotic.

We are marched to the camp Birkenau, part of Auschwitz, a few kilometers away. Then my mother, my sister, and me are taken to a place where we are stripped and our heads are shaven. Hair from all parts of our bodies is shaven. We did not recognize each other. You didn't know what you were doing. I was told to put my left arm out, there is no feeling anymore. And I am tattooed. 54090. My sister is 54091 and my mother 54092.

[Regina speaks directly to the interviewer:] You don't want to see it.

We were each given wooden shoes and a dress. You were lucky if the dress was big—then you had extra material to tear and make underwear. We are taken to our block, each one held a thousand women. The barrack welcomed us with fleas, like a plague. There were three layers of bunks, with six to a layer.

You'd think if you put people together in such terrible conditions, they would eat each other up. No—we fed ourselves with white lies of hope. We felt a closeness with the immediate group, because we were all from the same town. I was in the same block as my teacher, schoolmates, girlfriends, people I knew.

Every day, inmates were up at dawn, assembled in front of the barrack, and counted endlessly, without

food, shivering. Then the women were made to go to a
bare field where we faced barbed wire and the watchmen
in the towers. The ground had lime, and in the rain it
was all gray mud. Senseless orders were given. Only at
specified times could we go to relieve ourselves, but just
for a short time. Anyone taking too long was beaten off
the toilet. Evenings meant standing for hours and being
counted. Always counted.

We ate soup made up of water and weeds, and hard
bread that was flour and sawdust.

I had dysentery. My mother traded her bread ration
for coal, she'd heard that burned coal mixed with water
was a remedy. My mouth and teeth were black, but I
improved. Then there was lice and I got typhus, had a
high temperature. My mother and sister tried to help,
to hide my illness from being noticed. But I was sent to
the hospital. There was always the fear of never returning
from this place.

I climbed onto a bunk, a straw bed, which I shared
with a mother and daughter who were also very ill. I had
bedsores, which created a terrible burning sensation.
Soon I went into a coma. My mother came to visit me,
but I was not aware of it at the time, and have no memory
of how long I lay there—two weeks?

After, when I wake up, the girl beside me is singing
to her mother. "My mother sleeps better when I sing to
her," she said. I see that the mother is dead.

There is news that Mengele is coming to make a selection. Typhus patients were to be removed. I had a friend
who worked at the hospital and she told me to look good

for the inspection. She found a piece of red tissue paper and gave it to me. I rubbed my cheeks and tongue with it so to give them a healthy color. We were assembled, naked, before Mengele and his assistant. Mengele held a stick in his hand, only saying, "To the right, to the left . . ." He was handsome, like a frozen figurine, the look in his face had no feelings. Most were sent to the left. He points to me, "To the right."

The few of us who are remaining are sent out to the courtyard, and I see heaps of bodies, two stories high. Trucks come for those who were sent to the left. From many blocks, there are only enough people to fill one bunkhouse after the selection.

The next morning, my mother and sister find out that I have survived.

There were now new women in the camp, from different parts of Poland, and Greeks, Dutch, and Hungarians. The ones I had first come to Auschwitz with, from my hometown, had mostly died, few survived. The crematoriums were always going. Large transports of people were always coming.

I was given a striped uniform, red kerchief, and marched off to work in a block called "Canada." It was my job to sort the heaps of possessions taken from people once they had arrived in the camp: clothing, prayer books, eyeglasses, jewelry. . . . Sometimes, from a purse, you would find sugar or a piece of chocolate and eat it. It was a good position. I could smuggle out underwear and give it to a friend. I cried over the baby clothing we found.

Then one day there were no more Jews coming in. No more work to do but to sit in the block, be kicked or shoved. Someone, an officer, came looking for women to work on his farm in Germany. I was selected for this duty, but I did not want to leave my mother and sister. Then they were somehow able to make an arrangement to keep me from being taken far away, but it meant that I would be sent from Birkenau to Auschwitz. I would still be parted from them, but it was the best that could be done.

When I arrived, there were no jobs, only senseless work. Already it was the fall, soon it would be cold. I had friends who were working in the nearby munitions factory and they were smuggling out explosives, preparing for an uprising. A crematorium was blown up and the women involved were found out. Gallows was built. In October 1944, I witnessed this hanging. Life was very sad.

A few days before January 18, 1945, there was news that all of Auschwitz was to be evacuated. There was to be an enforced march. I wasn't well, my legs kept swelling. On the day of the march I heard that my mother and sister and the rest had been assembled in the morning and had left the camp. I was heartbroken. There was no way for me to find them. The panic in the camp was terrible, and I saw that the Germans couldn't keep count of the prisoners anymore.

With a few friends, I went to a block where there was a warehouse and hid under clothing, waited until dark. By night, most of the camp had been abandoned. The barrack was on fire and we ran to another to hide. We had heard some voices speaking Yiddish among the men putting out the fire. We hid for four more days without food or water. At night, we stepped out and ate snow.

One friend was very sick and we were worried she would die, so we left our hiding place. A German SS, with dogs, caught us, accused us of being spies. He took us at gunpoint to where there were other inmates, who were being made to destroy all the documents from the medical experiments that had been done at the camp.

[An interruption, a question: "Can you describe Liberation?"]

My only thought was escape and hide. Many of the German soldiers had already gone, run off. There were plans to blow up the barracks. We heard that the Jews would be blown up with the camp. German soldiers had gone to get the remaining Jews from Birkenau and bring them to Auschwitz. My friends and I dug under the barbed wire to go to the outskirts of the camp and wait to hear if the camp was to be destroyed. The soldiers were told to leave, to run from the Russians who were coming closer to the camp. We heard guns and knew it wasn't safe anymore to stay on the outskirts. I went back to the camp with my friends. We heard screams, roars, the Russians have come.

What can I tell you?

The Russian soldiers ask us what kind of place is this, what kind of prison. We explain it to them, tell them that many of us are sick, and the soldiers say, "You are free. Go home."

I become hysterical. We all did. We don't know how to rejoice. There is nowhere to go. But with my group, we decide to just leave. We leave for Cracow, we are several women and men. [My father is one of those men.] When we arrive, we tell people that we have come from a concentration camp, but no one believes us. We are hungry and are told to go to the monastery, for soup, for a place to sleep. I realize one has to try to survive even now.

The war was still going on. Our goal now is to go back home, to find others who have survived.

Near the end of February, we came to Katowice. My husband changed his name from Barek Eisenstein to Bolek Jurkowski. He took a Polish name so that he could enlist with the Bureau of Investigation of War Criminals, wanting to capture Nazis. He said he had been in a concentration camp, but not that he was Jewish. He was paid for his services, given food and lodging, and he did this for a couple of months. Jewish committees formed and relief was given. More people started to return. On May 10, there is news that my mother and sister have been on the Russian side and are coming back with the Polish army.

I cannot describe what it was like when I am reunited with my mother and sister . . .

This is where my mother finishes her story and the tape ends.

In 2002, my mother and my brother, Michael,
decided to join an organized trip back to the holy land,
back to Auschwitz. Yearly, groups are taken to the main
sites: Treblinka, Majdanek, Mauthausen, Auschwitz,
remaining synagogues, graveyards. We all felt such a sense
of proudness for my mother, in her resolve to return.

When they'd arrived in Auschwitz, they were led
through the grounds with a guide. As they entered one of
the barracks, my mother knew it was where she had been

and she recognized her bunk. She let the group continue on without her and she stayed behind alone. After, when she joined my brother and the others, a bus took them back to their hotel and she went to her room. That night, my mother became very ill. My brother told me how shaken he had been, seeing my mother so frail, realizing it had been a mistake to bring her back to this place that had caused her such harm. But the next morning my mother was able to continue on the trip, with interest and spirit. She is her own testament to survival.

I did not join them on this trip. My mother and my brother wanted me to be with them, but I had come to hate flying with a superstitious zeal that formed paralysis. Instead, the journey I took was a silent one later, when I sat and watched my mother telling her story on tape.

WHEN I FOUND THIS PHOTO RECENTLY, I COULDN'T BELIEVE IT. MY MOTHER, GRANDMOTHER, AND AUNT POSED AS I HAD WANTED TO DRAW THEM—SITTING CLOSE TOGETHER, WEARING WATCHES, THEIR NUMBERS IN A ROW. AFTER I FINISHED, I BRIEFLY SAW SOMETHING I'D NEVER SEEN IN THEM OR NEVER RECOGNIZED— A KIND OF INNOCENCE, A LIGHTNESS, AS IF THEIR ARMS DON'T EVEN CARRY THE MARK OF THE PAST.

I had not been there with my mother that night when she returned from her barrack in Auschwitz. I was not there to lie down beside her, be with her as she looked back—to the time when she hid with her family in Bedzin, before they are taken from their home, to the day her brother, Lemel, is separated from his mother and sisters, to the desolation and fear of believing she would never see her mother or her sister again. I wasn't able to make her feel safe, secure with my knowledge that her liberators would come.

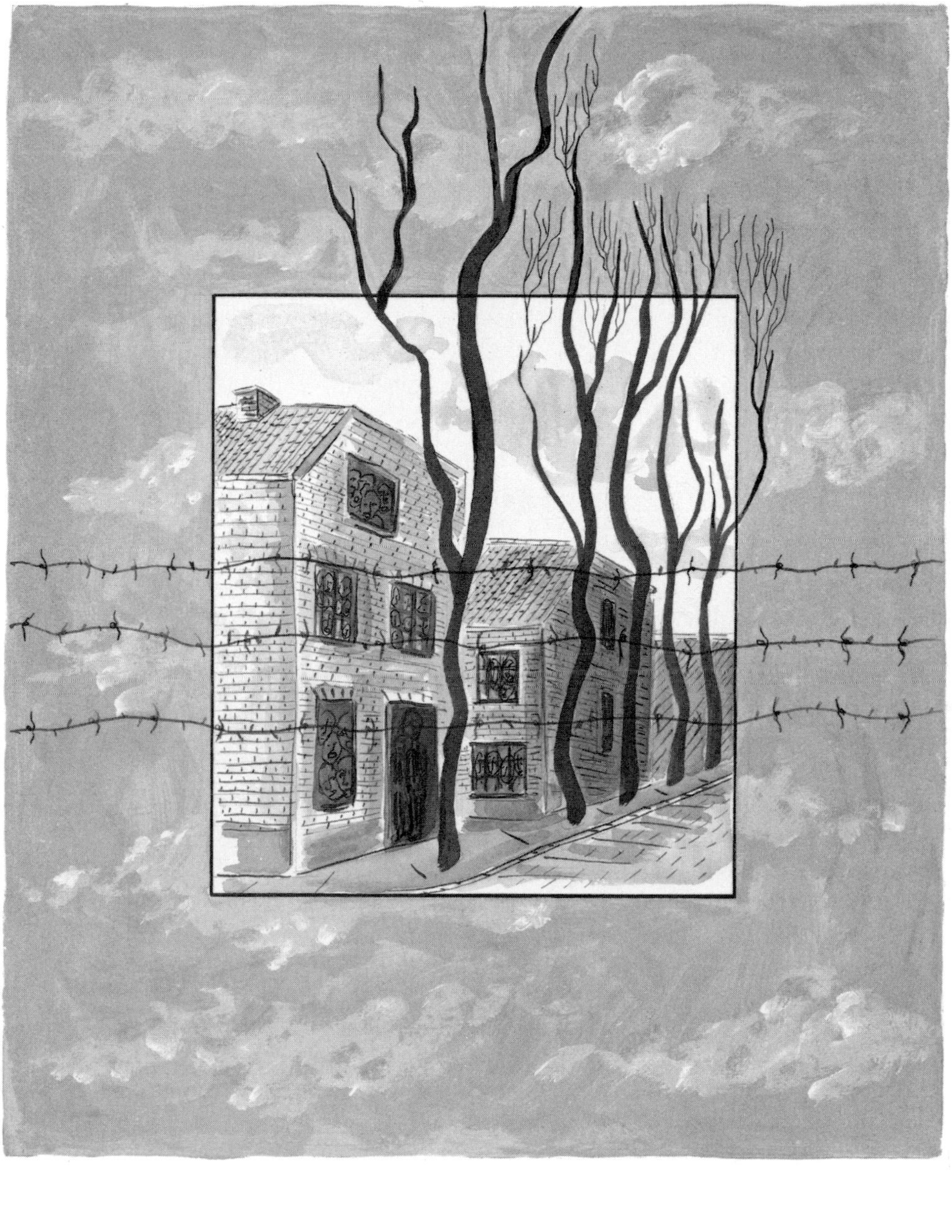

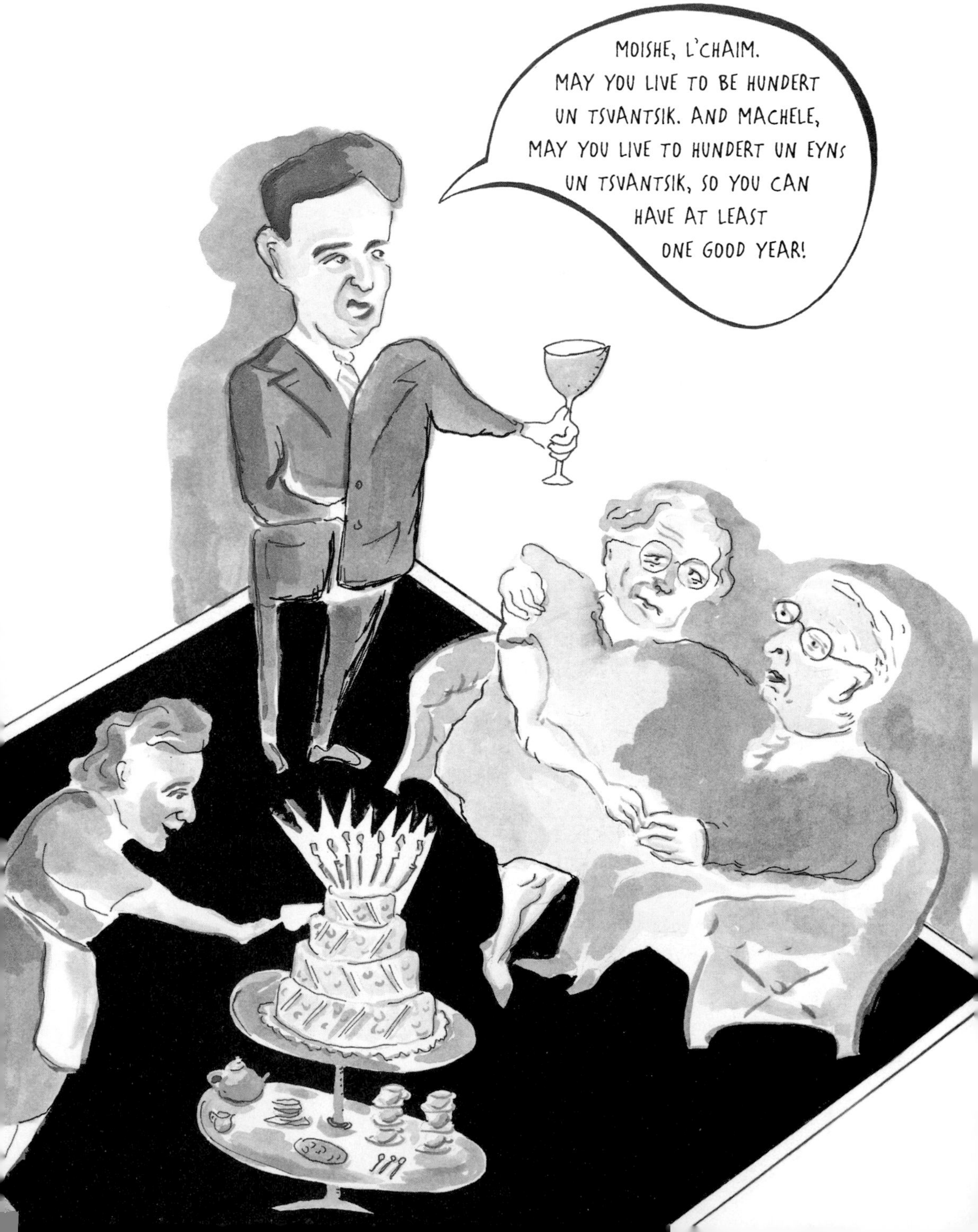
MOISHE, L'CHAIM. MAY YOU LIVE TO BE HUNDERT UN TSVANTSIK. AND MACHELE, MAY YOU LIVE TO HUNDERT UN EYNS UN TSVANTSIK, SO YOU CAN HAVE AT LEAST ONE GOOD YEAR!

I Was a Grandchild

My grandparents died twelve months apart from each other. He was ninety and she was ninety-one. My grandmother was once taller than her husband, but age had curved her spine, bending her forward. I remember her standing stooped over the candles she lit every Friday night before sundown, stooped over a kitchen sink or over a stove, preparing food to bring to her husband, making sure that he took another bite from the sponge cake she'd served him, saying softly, *Ess, Moishele*, eat. While my grandmother slowly turned inward with infirmity, my grandfather remained unchanged. He had only one position—seated. I could find him stationed in a plastic lawn chair on the small front porch of his house, on the couch in his den, or at the kitchen or dining-room

table. His deafness muted her utterances. His leaden pose, his fixed bearing, slowed her step to a standstill, until finally they lay side by side, blanketed by the decades they had lived together. I was never close to my grandparents or they to me. If they had been asked what memories they had of their grandchildren when they were young, they would have had little to say.

Shortly after my family left Braemore Gardens and moved to the suburbs, my grandparents, and my aunt and uncle with their two sons, joined the neighborhood. The three families each had their own homes, the interiors of which were decorated in similar fashion, reproduction Louis XIV, with sofas covered in plastic that not only recalled an era but stuck to your underside as you got up. The houses were copies in triplicate, but the Jewish traditions that were upheld within varied by degree. Although my father had been a kosher butcher for many years, my mother did not keep a strictly kosher kitchen. Unlike my grandparents and my aunt and uncle, we ate our meals off the same plates, mixing dairy and meat, though pork —and sadly, bacon— was forbidden, never allowed entry through the door. While our family and my aunt and uncle attended *shul* only on the High Holidays, my grandparents, who would be considered observant Jews, kept to the demands of the Sabbath and walked to the nearby synagogue every Saturday.

When I think back to each of these homes, I can recall certain sounds and the gesture of hands: My grandfather's fingers, always shaped into a molded fist; my grandmother's outstretched arms, which over the years drew in, forming a smaller embrace; the burning slap of my father's hand to my face, redeemed later by the firm hold of his protective arms. I hear my aunt's voice in her house as she practiced the Yiddish tunes she would later perform at a wedding or a bar mitzvah or at one of the many concerts held in synagogues and community centers around the city; hear the splash of water when my parents sometimes bathed together, the sound softening the remembered noises of their anger.

My grandparents' house was silent. My grandfather, Zayde Moishe, rarely spoke, but he had a way of harrumphing that defied classification. It came from deep down inside of him, churning like a volcano about to erupt, then shooting up and out into the air, landing bluntly on his own deaf ears. He *was* that harrumph. It punctuated his presence, reminding us that he was there in our midst, the eldest survivor, the patriarch of the family, though one from whom advice was never asked and no counsel ever offered. His daughters, my mother and my aunt, were always respectful and dutiful, and if they showed tenderness toward their father, it happened in privacy. It was his wife's unqualified devotion to him that somehow made up for the lack of everyone else's.

I should know more about this man. I should be able to bring something more into the room of his house where he sits surrounded by pictures of his wife and his two daughters and of the son he lost. Instead, I hold only a few words about him, spoken by my mother and by my aunt.

In the war, he had been taken from his wife and three children along with the other men from his home in Bedzin and was sent to a work camp. There he was beaten, and his hearing was left severely damaged from then on. After Liberation, with the aid of the Red Cross, he was sent to Sweden, as were other survivors, and was given medical care. He stayed on there and began a new life. My grandmother and aunt, still in Germany after the war, eventually were able to learn of his whereabouts. They obtained visas and reunited with him in Landskroner. It wasn't until my own father's funeral that I found out that after the war my grandfather had not looked to find his family, believing it was likely they had not survived. Perhaps when his wife and his daughter finally appeared before him, it was as if he were seeing their ghosts, telling him that his son, Lemel, had died in Auschwitz.

On the nights when my parents and my aunt and uncle worked late into the evening in their respective businesses, we ate dinner alone. Sometimes my grandmother prepared supper for her grandchildren, and on those occasions the stillness of my grandparents' house was set aside. Sharon and Michael and I, and our cousins, Michael and Larry, sat at the dining-room table with china plates carefully placed down on starched white linen and we *essed*.

Eventually, at some point, Michael and Larry, avid comic-book readers, would burst out with cartoon-balloon noises as they tossed imaginary explosive weapons back and forth across the table, proceeding to die in slow motion. My brother, sister, and I were grateful to be entertained, while my grandfather sat, deaf, not once looking up from his plate, and my grandmother kept serving more food.

At the end of the evening, my grandfather never rose from the table to see us to the door, which allowed my grandmother her private moment to press a quarter, a dollar, into our hands when she kissed us and said goodbye.

Toward the end of the 1960s, every fall my grandparents began to leave their house for an apartment in the sun, in Florida. Moishe would now have a warmer spot to sit and Machele would have fewer rooms to keep tidy. Every year, their Canadian home was left empty by November, safeguarded by the tenants who rented the basement apartment. Their plants were watered regularly, their kosher dishes remained undisturbed in the cupboards, and the couches in the den

AGE, NOT GRIEF, TOOK MOISHE WANDERING
DURING MY FATHER'S FUNERAL.

and in the living room stayed sealed with plastic covers, protected from dust.

The year I was twenty, I lived in Jerusalem, and when I returned to Canada, married, my husband and I initially stayed in my parents' house. We were both continuing our studies at university in Toronto. Not long before my grandparents left for the winter, I asked them if we might live in their house while they were away. I assured them that their home would be well looked after and that we would pay rent each month until they returned. My grandfather harrumphed in apparent agreement and my grandmother said that she would leave the key with my mother. On moving day, it took minutes to pack, books and clothing being our only possessions, and when I went to ask my mother for the key, she looked uncomfortable, then told me that my grandparents had changed their minds. She went on to say that they had decided to let my cousin Larry become their new tenant for free and that there was nothing more that could be done.

My mother accepted her parents' decision as a fait accompli not to be challenged, but with my father it was a very different story. I had never witnessed any exchange of warmth between my father and his *mechutonim*, his in-laws, and sometimes when he fought with my mother, the insult he'd hurl at her before leaving the room was to call her *akshen*, stubborn, like her parents. This time, my father boomed in fury, and for once I was glad. He let off some of the anger and hurt that I felt. *Es brent mir ahfen hartz . . . me hot a farshtopten kop . . . me drait zich vi a fortz in rossel!* I have heartburn . . . they're thick-headed . . . they squirm like a fart in a foggy soup!

My grandparents had slipped away to Florida, leaving my mother as the timid bearer of their decision. I knew they both had a great affection for Larry, who was named after their son, but in fact I was not all that surprised. I had never known my grandfather to be thoughtful or generous, or been asked by my grandmother to sit with her and talk so that she could find out who I was. They considered me rebellious and therefore unreliable.

Larry, a student at the downtown college of art, now had a new home, and I couldn't stay away. I had to go over and see how he was getting on in My Place. The house was unrecognizable. Every plate, meat and dairy, was out of the cupboards, some dirty in the sink, others just stacked on the counter, containing crusted bits of food, like forgotten Petri dishes growing some new form of mold not yet known to science. I'm convinced the cure for cancer lay there, smug and undetected. The furniture had been pushed to one side, supposedly to create more space for . . . for what? The dust? Every plant in the house was in the throes of death, leaves withered, stalks shriveled. Larry introduced me to his roommate (who gave him the right to become landlord?). He had befriended a fellow student, an Inuit, who was in need of a place to stay. I gasped, taking in the full display of chaos, and then watched my own breath hang in the air. Larry had turned off the heat in the house to cut down expenses. After all, it was winter.

How I wished for my grandparents to see their home now. *Oy vey iz mir.* Why has our chosen made such a *farkuck-teh* mess? But the wailing and the shrieking did not come to pass. In the end, my mother and my aunt cleaned up and put everything back in order before my grandparents returned, and Moishe and Machele went to their graves never knowing that their house, for a short while, had been a haven not only to their grandson but also to grime, mismatched dishes, and the True North.

My grandfather sat in a chair on his porch when he was ninety years old and had a stroke. In the hospital, he never awoke, and I watched him lying there on his bed, dying as he had lived—motionless. Ninety years upon this earth. Ninety years that carried unspoken the death of a son who, had he survived the war, would have been the one, according to custom, to honor his father's death: to go to daily services and to recite there the mourner's Kaddish for the obligatory year, thereby closing the circle of a Jewish life. Instead, an unknown *yeshiva bocher*, a seminary student, was paid to carry out this duty. Money that had always been so tightly held now served as the means to pay my grandfather homage.

The night before my grandfather was to be buried, the rabbi of the synagogue he had regularly attended for many years came to his house. He informed my grandmother that her husband had not purchased a plot, even when he had been given the opportunity, along with other founding members, to do so at a lesser fee. My grandmother asked him about making arrangements now for a double plot but was told that unfortunately most of the gravesites had already been spoken for and the best plots were no longer available. My grandfather was buried the next morning close to the curb of the road, where he lay alone for only one year.

And so my father's toast to my grandparents had become a prophecy, though he himself never lived to see this, his own death having occurred some time before theirs.

If I was unable to find a place in my grandfather's heart, my grandmother's, at least, allowed my approach. I have no memory of being taken into my grandfather's arms, but my grandmother's embrace was warm. It's hard for me to know how different my grandmother would have been had she not spent a lifetime with someone so closed off from the world. She had ministered without complaint all those years to the needs of her husband, bringing cups of tea to wherever he sat, making sure that he was comfortable and well fed. And all along she managed to partner his silence with a gentle voice, a gentleness that never revealed what she had suffered in the past.

I knew that my grandmother had hidden with her children until they were discovered and transported to Auschwitz, and that her son had died there. I had been told that in the camp she always tried to keep up her daughters' spirits and tended to their fears and illnesses. By the end of the war, when she was liberated, after surviving the march out of Auschwitz, she weighed seventy-five pounds. In all this, throughout my grandmother's life, from the early days of the war until her death, she held within herself the expression of what must have accompanied such loss.

What is owed to the story of their years if it cannot make memory yearn? It is impossible for me not only to have wished for more from my grandmother and grandfather but also for them, each in their own lives. I am unable to find the place where they were forever lost to themselves. Perhaps this is my grandparents' legacy to me.

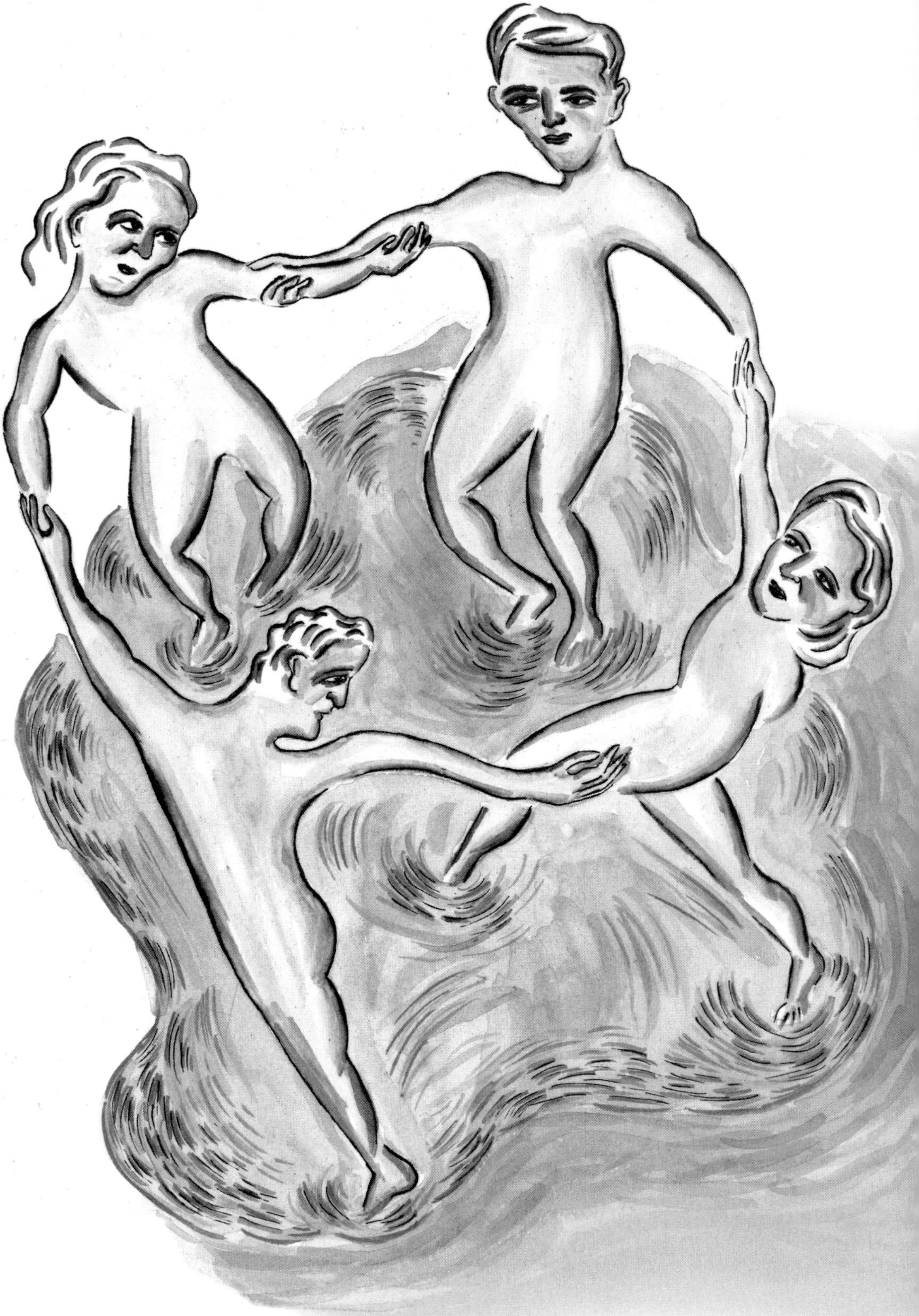

Two Brothers, Two Sisters

There is a Yiddish saying: A wise man hears one word
and understands two. I have no claims on wisdom, but
over time I have tried to consider things in more than
one way.

Take water, for example. Difficult to find if you're
wandering around in a desert, looking for an oasis,
but easy to believe within reach if the scorching sun
above your uncovered head has made you delirious.
The Bible gives it magical powers: you can walk on it,
use a lightning-struck rod to part it and let people pass
through, or wash away evil so that an ark can sail over it.
Greek mythology not only named the rivers of Hades but

also characterized them: Acheron was the river of woe; Phlegethon, the river of fire; Cocytus, the river of wailing; Styx, the river on which the souls of the dead were ferried; and Lethe, the river of forgetfulness.

Even philosophers don't make it any simpler for anyone choosing to get wet. Heraclitus believed that all things are in a harmonious process of continual change, summed up by the phrase: You can't step into the same river twice.

Water and memory both share the same elusive nature.

My father's brother, Jack, married Jenny, my mother's sister, and they became not only extended family but extensions of my parents' lives. And although my parents were only able to release scant drops of information from the flood of their own past, inevitably Jack and Jenny's history is found reflected there.

My uncle and his older brother, my father, were fortunate to have been able to stay together through most of the war. From the beginning, when the Germans moved the Jews of Miechow into a ghetto in the town, the two brothers were part of a selection of men sent to Rakowitz, an army base near Cracow. By the time Jack and my father were taken from the base two years later and brought to Plaszow, they'd found out that their parents and sisters had not survived.

I have never known precisely when or how they came to hear of their loss. My father did not speak about it, and I never thought to ask my uncle to provide more since I'd never discussed with him any of his experiences in the war. I have many times tried to imagine the sorrow that must have inhabited my father's heart, and now, oddly, in attempting to see my uncle clearly, it is the first time that I have considered what might have been in his.

Jack and my father remained in Plaszow for some time, having been passed over during the selections that occurred there with regularity, and after which prisoners would be shipped out of the camp, departing from one named hell to the unknown destination of the next. Then, in 1944, Jack and my father stood in line, one beside the other, during a selection. After the officer counted my father, he stopped, and from that moment on and for the rest of the war the brothers were separated. Jack was in Plaszow for a while longer, then sent on to another camp, where he was to stay until Liberation. He would not know until the end of the war that his brother had been taken to Auschwitz.

While envisioning the journey of two brothers, my own takes me to the parallel past of two sisters, their future brides-to-be, but not before they too become separated from each other.

Jenny and my mother, her older sister, and my grandmother were together in Birkenau until the point at which my mother was taken from the camp and transferred to Auschwitz, where she would remain for the rest of the war. My grandmother and aunt had somehow been able to prevent my mother from being sent to Germany on work duty but the outcome was still that they had to part. It would not be until May of 1945 that my aunt and my grandmother would reunite with my mother.

On January 18, 1945, Jenny and Machele would find themselves, along with thousands of others, being marched out of Birkenau to Auschwitz. The camp was in havoc, and Jenny and Machele tried to learn whether my mother was somewhere among the other prisoners, but they could not. Everyone was made to stand for hours outside in the cold until they finally left Auschwitz, on the death march. Jenny and Machele never knew that my mother was hiding somewhere in the camp and that she too had lost hope of finding them again.

My aunt once described to me the cold and the difficulty of walking on hard ground. Prisoners had torn pieces from what little they still had in the way of clothing and tried to cover their shoes. She saw people along the sides of the road, some already dead, others left to die there. Her one clear memory is from that first night, when in the dark she saw a sled in front of a farmhouse and quickly ran to steal it because her mother had barely enough strength to continue. Jenny spoke to another young woman whose mother was also failing, and together the two daughters pulled their mothers on the sled. The woman's father had already died, and after the war her mother came to remarry, a man who was first cousin to my grandmother.

My aunt went on to tell me how they traveled in railroad cars, without food or water, and that the walls were frozen with ice. When they arrived in Ravensbrück, they slept on the snow. From there, with other prisoners, they were sent to Neustadt Gleve, in Mecklenburg. On May 1, 1945, the Americans and the Russians arrived and the camp was liberated.

I did not want to press my aunt to go beyond what her memory allowed. And now I bring her and my grandmother to my mother, to when they finally reunited, in the Polish town of Katowice; to my uncle Jack, after he was liberated and made his way to this same town and found his brother again. The story is told that on the day he arrived, when he came to the building where my mother and father lived, Jenny was there sitting on the steps, polishing a pair of shoes. Jack walked up to her and asked if this was where his brother, Barek Eisenstein, lived. And then there would be two weddings.

My parents were the first to marry, and did so on June 24, 1945, in their small apartment in Katowice. Then, in August, they left Jack and Jenny and my grandmother and went in search of information about my mother's father. It was finally in Germany, in the

DP camp of Bergen-Belsen,
that my parents learned that
Moishe was recuperating in Sweden.
They sent word to Katowice, and Machele,
Jenny, and Jack joined them in Bergen-Belsen.
None of them had ever considered that Poland would
remain their home. Even though war had ended, the
country was still dangerous for Jews. Soon, my grandmother arranged passage to Sweden, for herself and her
daughter, and then a few months later Jack followed.
He and Jenny married and they and my grandparents
remained for some years in Sweden.

This was the last time the families would ever be
separated. My parents left for Canada in 1948, having
stayed in Bergen-Belsen for three years. Two years later,
my grandparents arrived in Toronto, followed by my aunt
and uncle, with their son, Michael.

*The first vivid memory I have of my aunt
comes from behind the heavy curtains of her
bedroom when I was four years old.* I had just
taken an amber-colored bottle from the nightstand
by her bed and, after squeezing drops of delicious
orange-flavored vitamins into my mouth, I peeked
out and watched my aunt breastfeed her newborn son,
Larry. Her jet-black hair covered her shoulders and
her pink skin spread into her baby's mouth.

I didn't come out of my hiding place to tell my aunt how beautiful she was, or ever let my uncle know that the way in which he greeted me when I was growing up, patting the top of my head and affectionately calling me "Topsy," is remembered to this day. As far as I know, *Uncle Tom's Cabin* has never been translated into Yiddish, but perhaps he had heard of the book and made me a character in *Uncle Jack's Shtetl*.

Over the years, I was in and out of my aunt and uncle's home and always their son Michael and I played together. He would be the first boy I held hands with and the first boy I kissed. When I was three years old and Michael was four, we asked my aunt if we could marry when we grew up. *Oy, a shkandal!* she said and went on to give us her Yiddish version of the birds and the bees. When kings married their cousins and made them queens, their children were *kuckamaimie*, cuckoo, their brains like *kashch*, porridge, and that's why the royal families of Europe were filled with so much *tsuris*, trouble. She finished off with: That's enough *kopdrayenish*, enough head-spinning non-sense. Michael and I laughed at her explanation. Even at this early age, we knew that we were already a *mish-mosh*— our aunts and uncles were brothers and sisters—and now one of *them* was setting *us* straight? We stopped kissing, but Michael and I continued to hold hands.

My aunt and uncle owned a clothing shop called Sara-Lee Fashions. Every day of the week they unlocked a door beneath the name that hyphenated their past: Sara for Jack's dead mother and Lee for Lemel, Jenny's lost brother.

MY AUNT FIRST SANG IN TORONTO IN A THEATER NOT FAR FROM OUR HOME
ON SPADINA AVENUE. BUILDINGS, TOO, SILENTLY KEEP THEIR HISTORY—THE
STANDARD BECAME THE STRAND, THEN THE VICTORY, LATER THE GOLDEN
HARVEST. THE MARQUEES ARE GONE NOW, AND TODAY A BANK STANDS
ON THE CORNER OF A BUSY STREET, THE PAST VAULTED AWAY.

When I was thirteen, I had begun to study oil paint-
ing and for a time I reproduced the works of the Great
Masters. Once, I painted a well-known Parisian street
scene, with shops lining the cobbled road, and wrote the
name of my aunt and uncle's business onto a storefront.
When I gave it to them as a gift, they proudly hung it in
their home, happy to have something that I had made
for them. I knew it would give them pleasure, especially
my aunt. I have always been aware that an interest in
music, books, and art has been central to her, sustaining
her spirit, and that this is something we have in common.

Over the years, I only stayed with my aunt and uncle
twice and, for different reasons, both occasions ended
unexpectedly. When I was six years old, my parents woke
me up early one morning, telling me that Uncle Jack
would soon arrive for me and that I was to stay at his
house for the weekend. My parents were driving to
Detroit to attend the wedding of a friend and my sister
and brother were going with them. I never understood
why they didn't take me with them and no reason was
provided, though if my parents did try to explain, I'm
sure that my loud wailing must have drowned out what
was said.

My uncle saw how unhappy I was and he and my aunt
did their best to make me comfortable, but I refused to eat
dinner that night and tried to persuade them to take me
back home. After all, we had a tenant in our house, a young
woman, and she could look after me until my parents
returned. They explained that they were responsible for me
and that I would only be with them for a couple of days.

The next morning, after foregoing another meal, I went with Michael to the park nearby and I remember staying sullen and miserable while we took turns going up and down the slide. Another boy soon arrived and then there were three of us on the equipment. The boy kept pushing ahead of me each time it was my turn. Michael asked him to stop, but when he didn't the two began to fight, rolling around in the sand. Michael became the first boy I ever loved.

OY GEVALT!

OY VEY IZ MIR!

On the way back home, he tried to convince me that he was all right, but his shirt was torn and the bruises on his face were swelling and turning color. Before we reached his door, he made me promise not to tell his parents that he had gotten into a fight.

I don't recall my aunt and uncle saying anything about Michael's appearance or know how they might have interpreted the evidence on his face. All I know is that soon after, they finally relented. Towards evening, Uncle Jack drove me back to my parents' house and left me in the care of the tenant. I was home.

I had never given much thought as to what my aunt and uncle were like as parents, raising their family, or whether they fought with each other in the same way my mother and father did. I didn't know if they were quick to anger or if they had greater patience with their own children than my parents seemed to have with theirs.

When I was fifteen, my parents agreed to send me to the scenic Muskoka region, north of the city, where my aunt and uncle, along with my grandparents, had rented a cottage for part of the summer. The area, filled with wooded expanses, lakes, and sandy beaches, is populated with summer homes. Michael and I spent our days at the beach. The only time we saw our grandparents was when we caught sight of them taking their regular stroll around the area, and my aunt and uncle stayed close to the cottage with their younger son, Larry. In the evenings, Michael and I played card games—hearts, rummy 500, poker, or clubbyish—and late into the night read the books we had brought. Summer in the country had determined an easy pace and it was lovely until, at some point, Michael and I made new friends.

We had met three other teenagers whose family owned a cottage nearby and we spent time with them at the beach over the next few days. Once Michael and I told his parents about our companions, the summer calm ended and suddenly everyone was upset. The people we had become friendly with were not Jewish, and what seemed to mean nothing to us meant everything to my grandparents and my aunt and uncle. We were forbidden to see them again. It was the first time I'd heard Michael raise his voice to his parents, and this incident was to be the beginning of a rift between them that would take years to heal.

The next day, my aunt stayed in bed, pale and feeling very ill. Michael and I spoke to her, not understanding what possible harm had been done. My aunt spoke about Auschwitz and pogroms and Hitler in one breath and then said that my father had been called to come and take me home that day.

At the time, I felt a mix of emotions, unhappy to be amidst a fury that Michael and I could not have fore- seen and angry towards my aunt and uncle's reaction. I remember wanting somehow to protect my aunt from the fears that spilled out of her, yet there was nothing that I could do or say. I did not feel as if an apology was owed.

Michael and I had opened up a Pandora's box and the strength of what flew out overwhelmed us. And an earlier warning was brought back, my aunt speaking to us once as small children, lightheartedly, but this time it was eerily different. After the war, the Jews of Europe had become an endangered genetic pool and, tragically, my aunt knew too well the guardianship needed to ensure its renewal.

I had visited my uncle in his home not long before he died. We played a few hands of cards for a short time while my aunt straightened the bedroom, tireless and unwavering in her will to take care of her husband. When my aunt left the room to bring back some food she had prepared, my uncle told me that he had no appetite and that the only reason he ate was so that his wife could get some rest.

People are harshly uprooted and separated from the safety they have made of their lives, by circumstance or by loss, by time, and now my father and my uncle are gone, leaving two sisters with the comfort of each other's company. When my mother turned eighty recently, we invited friends and family to join us in celebration. She received bouquets of flowers and cards and was presented with a framed certificate from the Women of the Zaglembier Society, in recognition of the charity work she has done over the years. She sat in a chair as she was serenaded in Yiddish by a few of her friends. Later, after several speeches, my mother wanted to say a few words. She stood and looked around the room, at the people surrounding her, and thanked everyone for coming. Although we had many times heard my mother's ease in expressing her gratitude and warmth, we were unprepared for what she went on to say. She said that half her life had been broken, and then her husband died, and that what she wanted now was to remain strong, for her family. She spoke from her heart, of her deepest feelings, and was poignant in the brevity of her words. And then it was time for my aunt to speak.

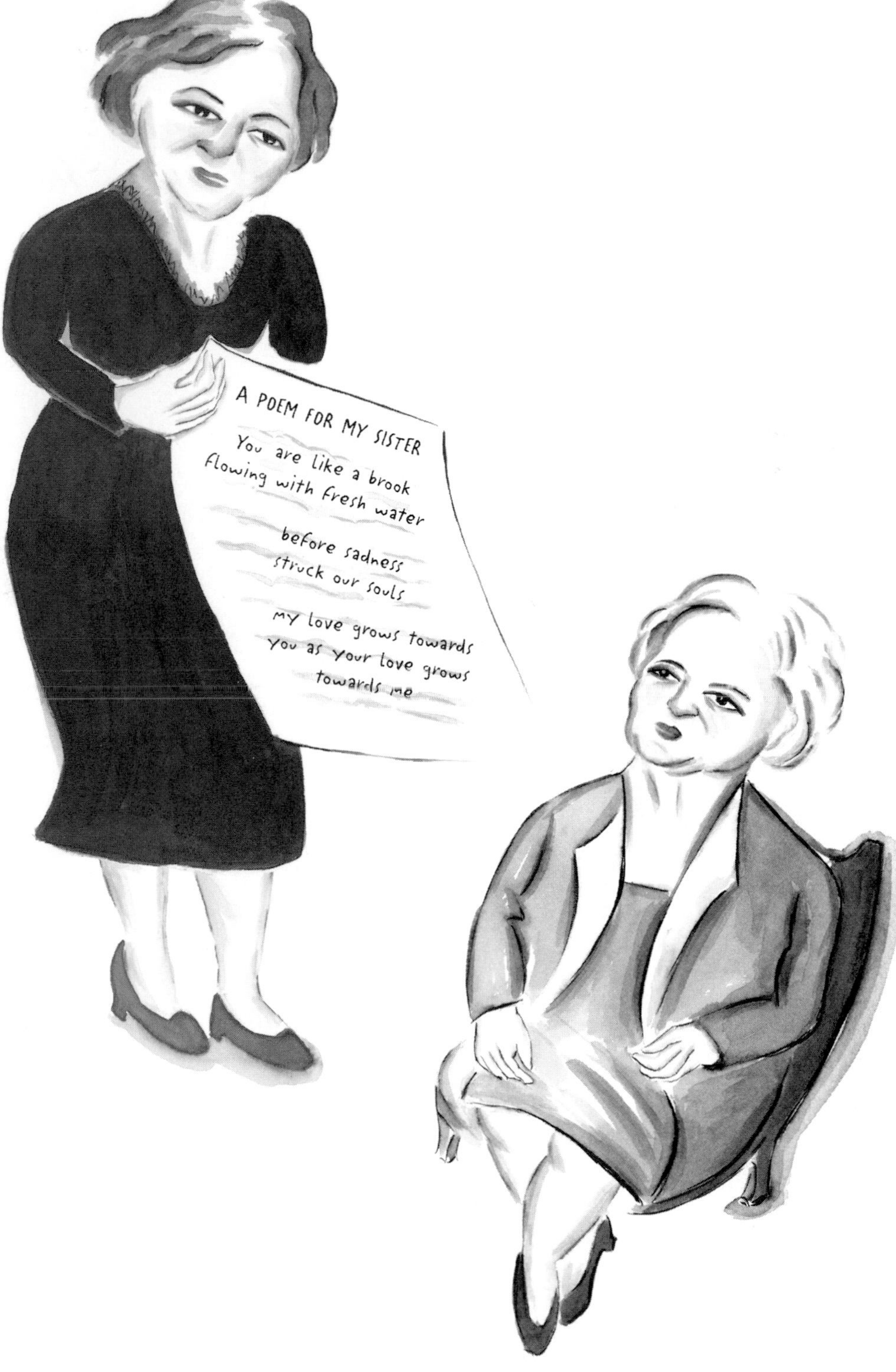
A POEM FOR MY SISTER
You are like a brook
flowing with fresh water
before sadness
struck our souls
MY love grows towards
you as your love grows
towards me

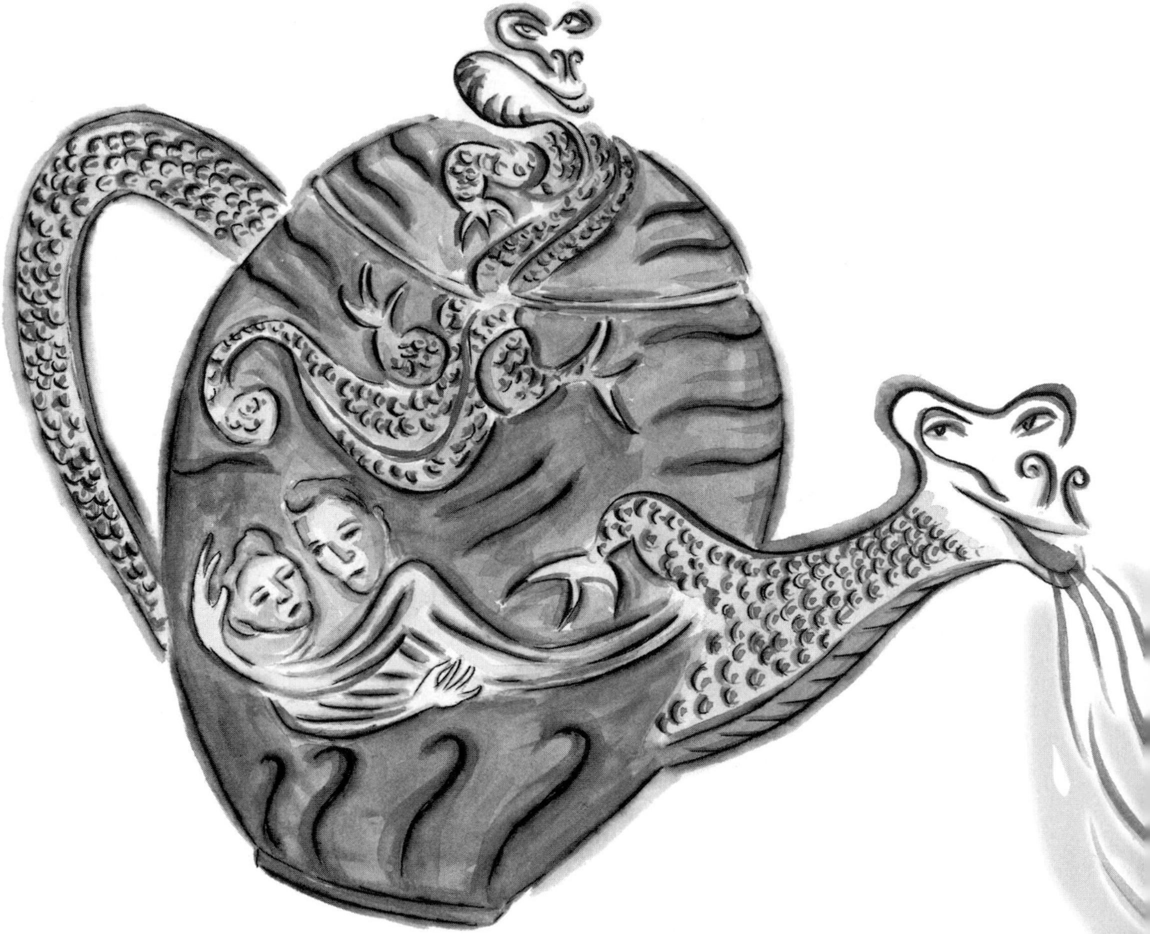

The Glass Cabinet

My parents came to Canada with few possessions. There
was a large porcelain elephant, with an ear that had been
chipped and later crudely remolded. A graceful figurine
of a naked woman with one arm delicately outstretched,
holding an orb; the other hand, at her side, was missing
some fingers. Several cups and saucers rimmed in gold,
with images of kings and queens painted on the surface.
The body of a dragon wrapped around a teapot completed
the set, with its neck and head forming the spout, and
instead of fire, tea flowed out of the dragon's mouth.
These objects they had brought with them from Europe
would eventually be placed inside the glass-fronted cabinet
that was part of my parents' new dining-room suite.

I remember a large chandelier, strung with pieces of faceted glass, hovering over the dining-room table, radiating an intense heat. Fortunately, a chain hung down from its center that could be pulled to adjust the level of wattage produced. Often this was the initial spark that stirred conversation: Dim the light. It's too bright, pull the chain. No, now it's too dark, I can't see what I'm eating. But whatever degree of light dimmed or brightened the dining-room table, this is where we ate during the High Holidays or when celebrating a birthday and where Passover seders with the family were held once my grandmother grew too tired to stand over a stove, preparing the many dishes.

No matter what the special occasion, my mother took full advantage of her extensive culinary repertoire. She'd make gefilte fish, sweet, not peppered, a sinus-clearing horseradish, and gallah—a jellied concoction derived from boiled calves' feet and more like Aspic of Nothing. Its plain appearance would sometimes vary, with a hard-boiled egg or pieces of garlic suspended inside. Once people were seated around the table, the door between the kitchen and the dining room was in continuous full swing as my mother walked in and out, placing platters of food onto an already overladen table. Eager to satisfy everyone's palate, she served two kinds of *lokshen kugel*, noodle pudding, one sweet with raisins, the other savory and salted. Roasted potatoes arrived, sprinkled with pieces of fried-crispy fat, *greben*, the crème de la crème of artery-hardening foods. And we loved it! Then trays of meat were paraded out: turkey, roast beef, and chicken, fried, baked, and boiled. Designer waters had not yet been invented, so to wash it all down we drank *suda wasser*, soda water, and lots of it. Soda water used to appear off the backside of a truck, delivered once a week in a wooden crate and placed neatly in our garage. There was a cylinder attached to the neck of each bottle and squeezing the lever released carbon dioxide into the water, making it effervescent and providing diners with intermittent relief. My father, who ate happily at these feasts, drank gallons of it, *shpritzing* soda water to the top of his glass, always wetting the tablecloth. Once I learned more about the Holocaust, the idea of gassy water made me think about Jews standing in line, waiting to be showered. But there was no Zyklon B in the cylinder. It was just *suda wasser*.

After the main course was eaten, the dishes were removed, making room for a compote of stewed prunes and apricots and what was to follow. Platters of cake and cookies, fruits and nuts, were brought out by my mother, who had never managed to sit down and actually eat with us even though we asked her to join

ZERO MOSTEL WAS ONCE OVERHEARD TO PASS CULINARY JUDGMENT IN A NEW YORK DELICATESSEN WHERE GREBEN WAS SERVED.

THIS RESTAURANT HAS KILLED MORE JEWS THAN THE HOLOCAUST!

us, to rest for a minute, and enjoy what she had prepared. Mom, you made too much food, we'd tell her. But she'd just smile, look at everyone around the table, all of us weighted down with what we'd consumed, and, with great pride, say, Thank you.

I can see my father sitting as always at the head of the table with the glass cabinet behind him. On Passover, he would read from the Haggadah solemnly, and sometimes quickly. As it happens, the first night of Passover occasionally coincides with the hockey playoffs, and during those seders, the Egyptians would get off light as my father rushed through the Ten Plagues and hurried the Jews through parted waters and into their Promised Land so that he could go up to his bedroom and watch the hockey game.

While we continued with dessert, we could hear him in the bedroom, yelling: *Er kricht vi a vantz,* He's slow as a bedbug, the words thrown at a player who had missed the puck. *Er macht a tel fun dem,* He's ruining it, *er toyg ahf kapores,* he's worthless. And if the player didn't improve, he was insulted further. *Er zol vaksen vi a tsibeleh, mit dem kop in drerd,* He should grow like an onion, with his head in the ground. Hearing this, my mother says to those around the table, *Er zitst oyf shpilkes,* He sits on pins and needles.

I remember on one particular Passover evening when that night became different from all the rest. After the meal, my father stood, turned to the cabinet, and opened its door. Recently, several more pieces of porcelain had been added, joining the others on the shelves. My father had purchased a set of ceramic monkeys, Meissen figurines, with each animal dressed in Renaissance costume and holding a musical instrument. He reached in, carefully taking out one of the prized figures, and held it out proudly—a monkey with a baton in his raised hand, poised to conduct his band. My father was unusually spirited that night. He told us how finely crafted these figures were and how much pleasure it gave him whenever he looked at them. After he returned the conductor to its place, he picked up the porcelain figurine of the woman, and looking at it for a moment, he was reminded of another time. He began to speak about his life after the war, after Liberation, when he and my mother lived in Bergen-Belsen as displaced persons.

War ends and my parents are liberated, and over the years all that I have ever been able to imagine is chaos and sickness and exhaustion and the constant rediscovery that so few survived. But I was wrong. There was more. Life forces life to continue.

My father talks about the canteen he ran in Bergen-Belsen. He said he knew that if cigarettes or bags of coffee could be bought cheaply from the black market and sold for a profit, he would have a few dollars more

ON APRIL 15, 1946, ONE YEAR AFTER BERGEN-BELSEN'S LIBERATION, MY FATHER MARCHED ALONGSIDE OTHERS TO THE MASS GRAVES.

to buy scraps of gold. He would then take these to a trusted jeweler, an alchemist, who would transform them into the currency that would help my father make his way out of Europe. He tells of how he frequently left the camp and traveled to Hanover, from there journeying by train the four hours to Cologne, returning the next day to his wife, who was by this time pregnant with my sister, Sharon. Once, in Cologne, he was picked up by the police for black-marketing and taken to headquarters, where his bag of illicit trade was confiscated. He showed his papers, told them that he was living in Bergen-Belsen, and that he and his wife were expecting a child. He promised that if they let him go then, he would come back on the date that had been set for his hearing, and the police released him on his word.

Two weeks later, he returned to Cologne and entered the court building. He stood outside the courtroom with others who, like him, had been picked up for black-marketing. While waiting, a man appeared, wearing the robes of a judge, and he and my father recognized each other. My father explains that the man had been sent to Auschwitz earlier in the war for his political views and that they'd met when my father arrived there in 1944. They embraced. Barek, what are you doing here?

Once my father told why he was there that day, the judge instructed the other officials that the police were no longer permitted to arrest Jews for black-marketing and that he never again wanted to see a survivor standing before him in his courtroom. My father pauses here, briefly. His blue-gray eyes, vivid, were fixed on the distance, illuminated by a moment from his past. Afterwards, he tells us, they shook hands, wished each other well, and parted. His story over, he placed the figurine back on the shelf, closed the cabinet, and sat down, contented and relaxed.

I think of my father as someone who had difficulty expressing himself through language, but that night he recounted his story fluently and with excitement. I had watched his face as he spoke and I saw the look in his eyes as he stepped back to a place that had been transformed, to a time when he and my mother and those who were there with them began to live. He had given me a compass with which I could find my way to where he wanted his own memories to begin.

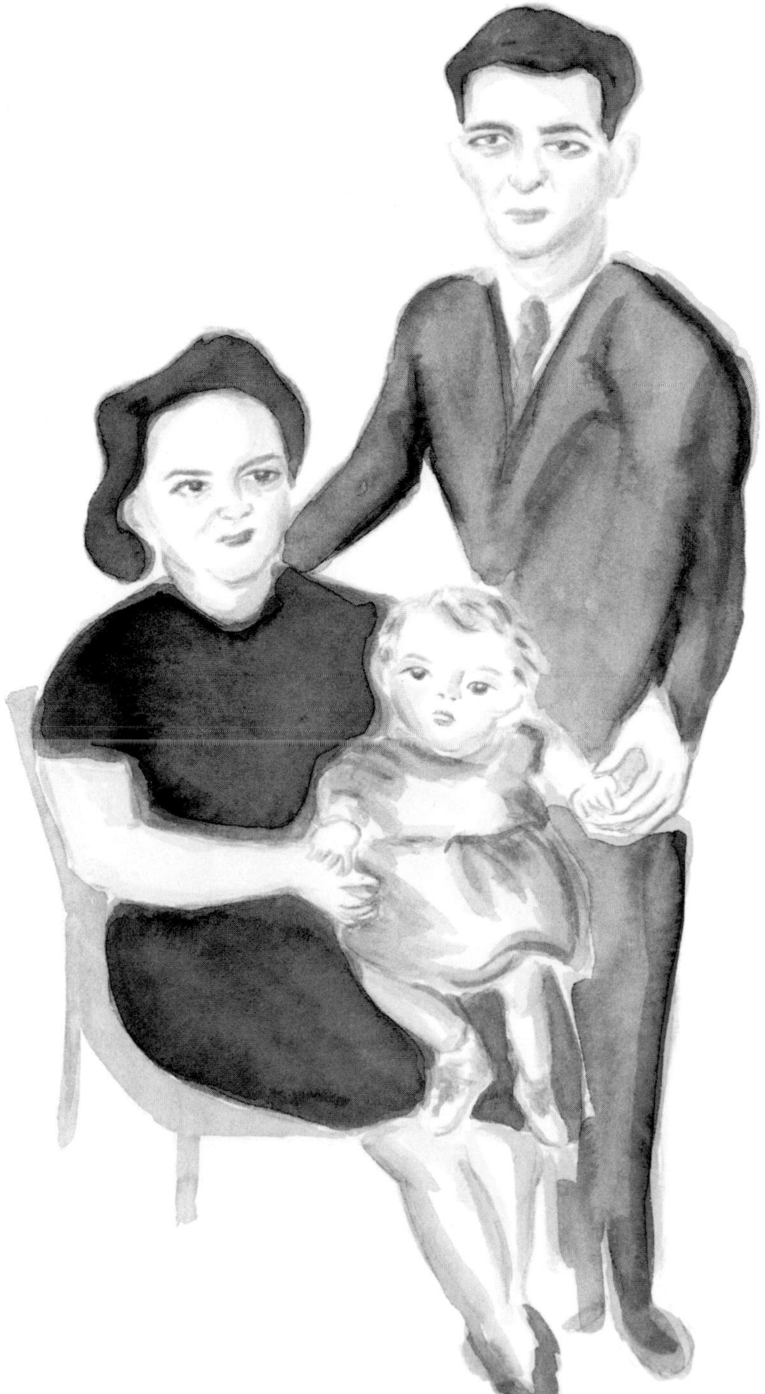

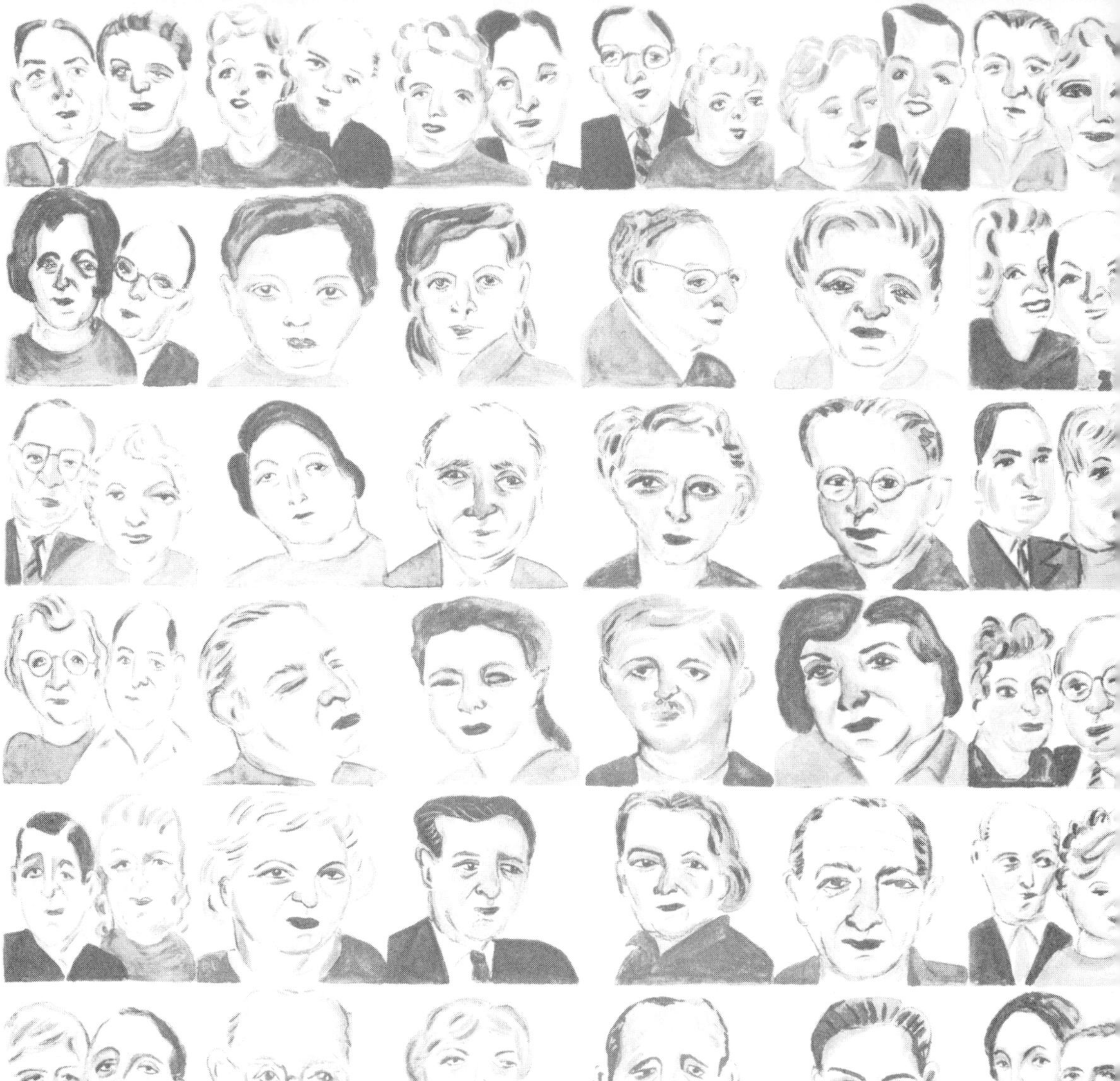

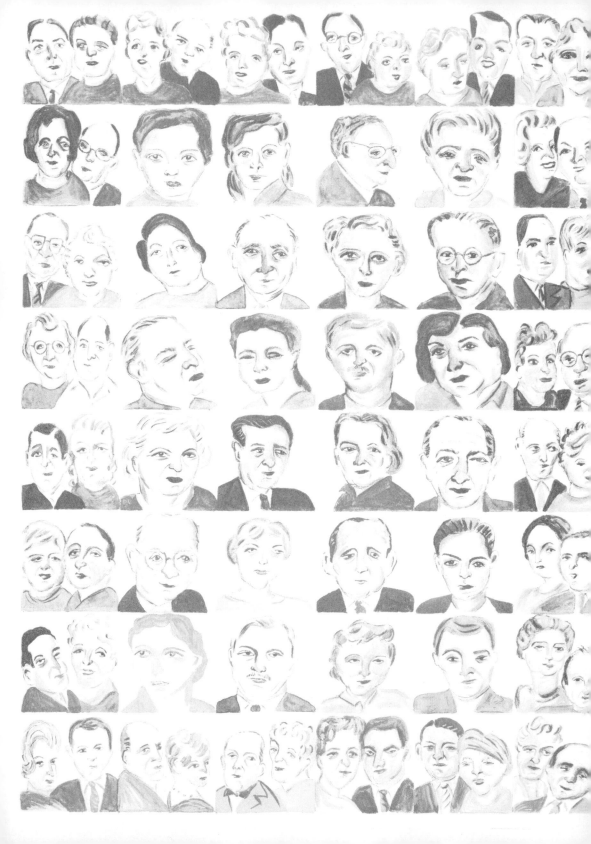

The Group

A Rose by any other name is Rooshka, Chana, Hanka, Dorka, Monka, Monia, Mania, Tonia, Anja, Jadzia, Chemya, Heniek, Moniek, Srulek, Bolek, Barek, Rishu, Reginchka, Lalushka, Doovidle, Bella, Hela, Yisrool. . . . As a child I sometimes chanted these names over and over again. The sounds swirled into my ears and have remained there all these years.

My parents' friends, the Group, were always together: playing gin rummy and poker on Saturday nights, picnicking in parks on weekends during the summer, attending bar mitzvahs, weddings, a *bris*, a luncheon, teas, fundraisers. They shared cottages, vacations—you name it, they did it together. They had all known one another in Europe.

Most were from my parents' hometowns or had grown up in the neighboring area, but all of them were linked to the same past, sharing the same history, an unbroken chain of survivors. Whenever the Group got together for an event or a social occasion, there was always the air of a reunion being held. They adhered one to the other with the kind of bond that would be hard to duplicate—at times, it felt, even with their own children.

I remember most vividly the bar mitzvahs, and I attended many while I was growing up. The event was always captured on film, and when viewed at a later date it unreeled like a silent movie, with everyone's movements slightly speeded up, jerky, and awkwardly spliced together.

There's the receiving line, with the proud parents and their today-I-am-a-man son standing side by side, shaking hands, being hugged and kissed by the guests. Family and friends arrive—gowned, sequined, bejeweled, bedecked. There is a table set with place cards for guests to discover where and with whom they are seated. Always, someone is flustered, upset that they are to dine at the same table

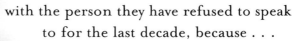

with the person they have refused to speak
to for the last decade, because . . .
well, they just can't remember,
but still the memory of the
insult remains. *Oy gevalt,*
but it's a *simcha,* and the
injured party takes his seat.
Look—it's Norman and
Rose. They've come all the
way from Detroit, *Michigass—*
Michigan. He has his arm around his wife and they're
laughing. Just back from Florida, they are both evenly
tanned. Norman had a wife and a young child before the
war but they died in a concentration camp. Now he sits at
the table, weightless in his tuxedo, content and pros-
perous, with his wife and their two sons and his friends.
Rose puts a hand to her lacquered hair, making sure
that the architecture on top of her head hasn't shifted.
Comforted by the tactile assurance that hairspray defies
gravity, she takes out a lipstick from her sequined bag
and retouches red to her lips so that the brush of her
affections leaves a trace. Rose is the friend who saved my
mother's life with a piece of paper when they were both
in Auschwitz. It was she who had brought red tissue to
my mother, who was ill, so that she could rub color into
her cheeks and be spared.

Fabian and Nadja are seated next to them. Nadja is
wearing one of the many knitted outfits she creates. Like
Madame Defarge in *A Tale of Two Cities,* she was always knit-
ting and purling, styling herself and her two daughters in

Coco Chanel knockoffs. Nadja looks after her husband's attire as well, straightening his bow tie, brushing invisible fluff from his jacket, smoothing his graying hair. Pencil thin, she is tall and elegant. Fabian is short and squat and his suits always seem oversized, with the cuffs a little too long, the pant legs too close to the ground. Fabian spent most of the war in hiding, and when I first learned this from my father as a child, I always wondered whether living so long in the dark had prevented his growth. After the war, he and Nadja lived in Paris for a few years before immigrating to Canada. Their daughters are thin like their mother, both sickly and shy. Fabian is my father's best friend and will be the first one from the Group to die. He will have a heart attack and leave Nadja alone to worry about the future of her girls until Alzheimer's erases that load and leaves her to spend her days sitting, waiting, no longer able to knit. My mother and aunt will visit her in the seniors' home and when Jenny sweetly sings a Yiddish tune, Nadja awakens and joins in the notes of their past: *"Azoyfil lider hob ikh gehert, / Nor ale hobn mir deresn. / Nor eyn lid iz mir geblibn, / En ekh ken im nisht fargesn, / Oy vey, kh'ken im nisht fargesn. . . .* I've heard so many songs, / But I've tired of them all. / One song alone has stayed with me, / And I can't forget it, / I just can't forget it. . . ."

Nadja leans back
in her chair and
laughs, then stands
up and puts her
arms out to her
husband and
together they
make their way
to the dance
floor. The
band is playing
a cha-cha, their
favorite, and
they move back
and forth, nodding
to other dancing
couples as they pass,
in perfect rhythm with
each other.

Now Harry and Bella
have just come over to the
table to say hello to their friends.
He too is shorter than his wife. Bella's fleshy cheeks are
powdered with rouge, granting her a soft glow of health,
and the rings sparkling on her fingers will be taken off
that night with difficulty. Eventually her body will be
crippled by arthritis and the canes that assist her walk
and the steroids that relieve her painful steps will both
ultimately fail. And when she dies, the Group will never
let go of her memory.

She holds her husband's hand as they return to their table and he pulls out the chair for her, deftly gliding it in just as she sits down, then puts his lips to her cheek. Harry looks forward to the end of the evening when he can return to the book he has been reading. He takes great pleasure in privately pursuing his education. Whenever Harry comes to our house, he is always curious about whatever book I am reading, and his questions, spoken in a soothing voice, draw me out of my shyness.

Carola turns to talk to Harry beside her. Several years younger than the others in the Group, she looks lovely in her tightly fitted brocade dress. Trim and lithe, she has always been light on her feet, her quick steps barely noticed. On the transport from Miechow to Treblinka, Carola was able to jump from the moving train, falling away not only from her family but from my father's as well, and from all the others whose lives entered darkness once the doors had been sealed.

The dinner has been served and it's time for a friend to say a few words. David lifts his heavy body from his chair. His wife, Helen, stays seated, and gazes up proudly, knowing that this is her husband's most enjoyable moment of the evening. He makes the toast at all the gatherings, imagining himself as the shepherd of his flock, instructive and protective. David clears his throat, raises his wineglass, and looks over to the long table where the celebrating family sits. His words are spoken effortlessly, the emotion matching the deep timbre of his voice: "*Meine freynde*, my friends, a toast to the bar mitzvah boy, who we have all known since he was born. And to his

parents, our dearest friends. May we all continue to have
good health, *biz hundert un tsvantsik*, till a hundred and twenty,
and be together as we are here tonight, celebrating *simchas.*
Our children, our *kinderlach*, should never know the hard-
ships we have endured. To all their lives and to all those
who are not with us now, to life, *l'chaim!*"

   The band knows its cue, and at the very moment
David sits down, Aunt Jenny, already on stage, belts out
a lively rendition of the song "To Life," from *Fiddler on the
Roof.* Everyone joins in, but David is quiet, overcome with
emotion, and Helen puts her arm
around her husband. His
bulk will diminish over the
years and confusion will

keep him from finding the same words of well-wishing as he ages. Never wanting to be separated, Helen and David will die in quick succession of each other and the *shivah* that takes place in their small house will hold all those children he blessed over the years.

The dessert table now on display, a Siren call of sweets, is proof that the art of culinary creation is limitless. A lifelike ice sculpture of the brrr mitzvah boy slowly melts in the center of the table. A watermelon, hollowed out and carved into the shape of the *Exodus*, the ship that brought refugees to the Land of Milk and Honey in 1947, is filled with new bounty—melon balls. A large platter offers a mountain of vanilla-flavored pareve ice cream, made from (in)edible oil products, since roast beef was the main course and thou shalt not mix meat and milk at a meal. And this isn't just any mountain, it's Sinai, topped with a chocolate mold of Moses holding the Ten Commandments. Nearby, the Red Sea as Jell-O jiggles, with puff-pastry Egyptians floating inside, just desserts for all

the trouble that was caused so long ago. Then there are the decorated cakes: a sponge cake, noted for the height that whipped egg whites can attain, is the Tower of Babel, and circling its base are candied prophets foretelling of doom. A hazelnut cake in the shape of the Star of David is edged with tiny blue-and-white Israeli flags. Scattered across the table are hundreds of glazed petit fours, decorated on the theme of the Garden of Eden with little animals, palm trees, flowers of every variety, the Tree of Knowledge, fig leaves, snakes, apples, multiple Adams and Eves in various poses. . . .

Uncle Ella, my grandfather's brother, jumps to his feet, and as he makes his way to the decorated offerings, he passes the bar mitzvah boy. They are both the same height and size. Ella takes an envelope from his pocket and simultaneously hands the gift to the boy and pinches his cheek as hard as possible, the kind of pinch where flesh is not only grabbed but twisted. "*Mazel tov*, congratulations." Ella's wife and child died in Auschwitz, and after the war he moved to Palestine, where he married Shifra, and together they came to Canada and raised two sons and a daughter. Like Noah of the sweet table, following God's direction, he selects two of every dessert to bring back and share with his wife. He is beaming with excitement, for he loves attending every one of these events, surrounded by family.

The hired photographers have done their job well, archiving the celebration on film. Clothing styles and hairdos never seem to change. Hair is swept up high, sprayed and sparkled, all versions of a tidal wave just

before it hits the shore. Gowns remain ornately sequined
and will later be plastic-wrapped and hung in a cedar
closet, waiting to be taken out for the wearer's appearance
at some other occasion.

*I have come to understand, in a way less
known than felt, something of what my parents
and their friends have meant to one another,*
and realize why it had always been impossible for me not
to have sensed myself an outsider. If for five years they
were herded—*arous*—en masse into cattle cars, separated
from their families, bunkered in suffocating quarters,
marched from one camp to the next, all that was left as
a final solution was each other. They were one another's
home, their own having been confiscated and destroyed.

My parents and their friends are inextricably linked, by the events in their shared past and by the future they came to build. And while I knew from an early age that I did not possess the particular magnetism that would draw my parents to me, the pull of their history was irresistible. I think in some way I have always been able to step into the presence of absence. It is something that I have needed to do. But I have never found for myself the right distance from the time when their lives had been so damaged.

Without my family's knowledge or even their understanding, their past has shaped my loneliness and anger, and sculpted the meaning of loss and love. I have inherited the unbearable lightness of being a child of Holocaust survivors. Cursed and blessed. Black, white, and shadowed.

Once I became older and left home, stepping into my own life, the occasions when I saw my parents' friends became less frequent, and in recent years have centered around the High Holidays. A few days before Yom Kippur, there is always a memorial Yizkor service held at the Zaglembier Society's funeral grounds at the north end of the city. This is where my father and my uncle are buried. It is also filled with tombstones that have been engraved with the names of others from the Group who have died. Their stone garden grows. During the service each year, I stand with my mother and my brother and sister, listening to solemn words spoken about the importance of remembrance, sentiments I have heard all

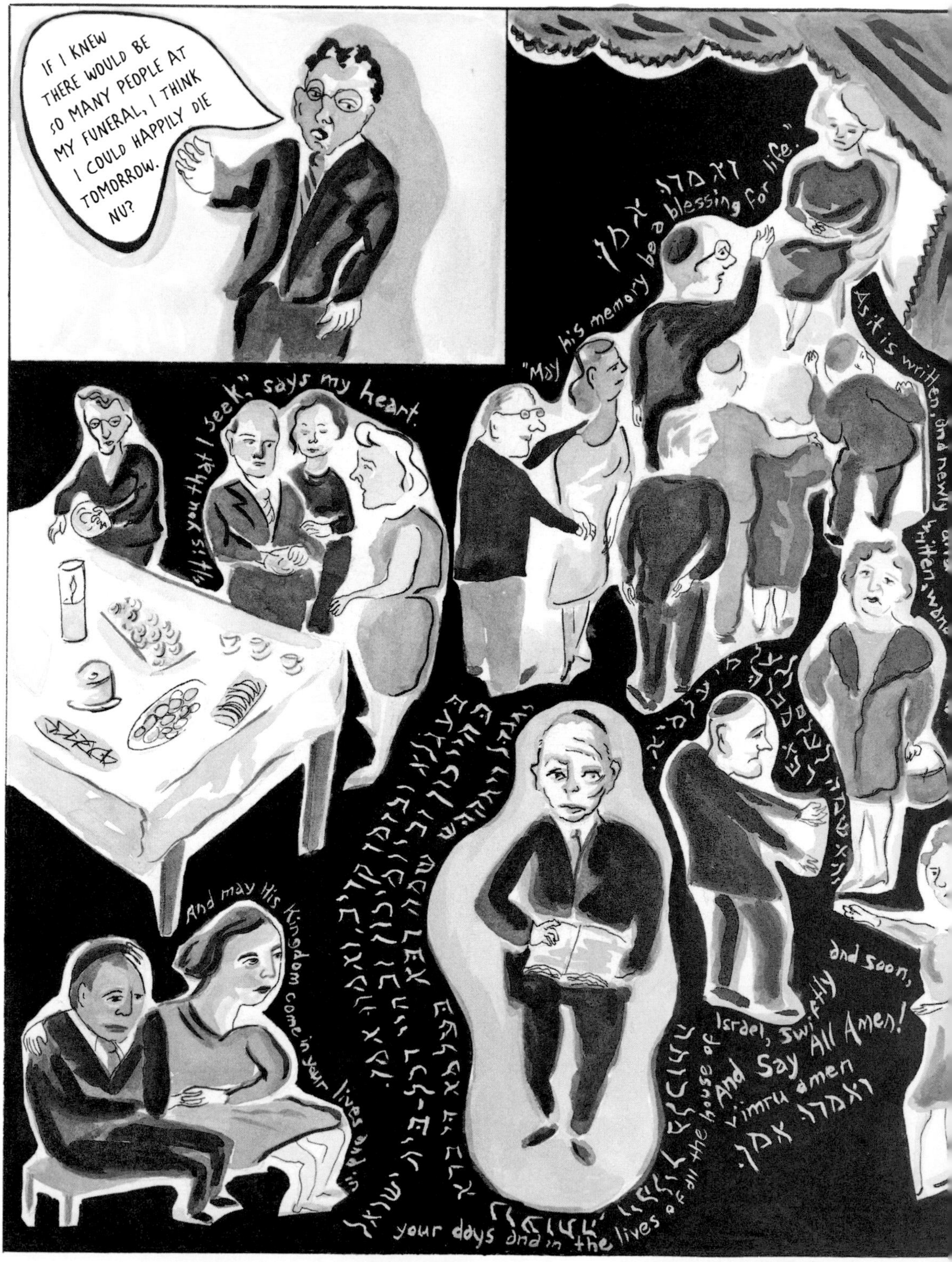
IF I KNEW THERE WOULD BE SO MANY PEOPLE AT MY FUNERAL, I THINK I COULD HAPPILY DIE TOMORROW. NU?
"May his memory be a blessing for life."
is you that I seek," says my heart.
As it is written, and newly written,
And may His Kingdom come in your lives and in your days and in the lives of all the house of Israel, swiftly and soon,
And Say All Amen!
v'imru amen

my life. Afterwards, I warmly embrace my parents' friends, missing those who are no longer present, and then I join the company of the *kinderlach*, the children of the Group, whom I played with when I was young, children who like myself have been adults for quite some time. But these isolated occasions have become diminished for me some-how, and are unevenly threaded together in memory.

I have my parents' albums now, filled with photographs of the Group huddled tightly, sitting around tables, or dancing, everyone always with a smile whenever they got together. In some photographs, the color has faded; in others, more recent, the gathering has become noticeably smaller. The tight hold they've had on one another has been loosened as they have aged.

At the end of June, a few years ago, my husband and I decided to drive to New York City, spend a week there, and then make our way back through the picturesque Berkshire Mountains in Massachusetts. Not long before we left, my mother mentioned that her good friend Bluma, who wintered in Florida, had a summer cottage in the Catskill Mountains, in Monticello, New York. She suggested that on our return home we might spend a night there, and that if we liked she would be happy to call Bluma.

I thought back to the summers when I was young, when the Group rented several cottages at Wasaga Beach, an hour and a half's drive north of Toronto. During the week, the men stayed behind in the city tending to their businesses and on weekends they joined their families.

The children made up their own group and were largely unattended, free to play and swim at the beach till the sun set, baking till we blistered. The water was famous for its far-reaching sandbars, and our parents, not thinking about the deep waters that lay beyond, must have thought we would be safe if we swam out from the shore. Lucky for them we had already learned from their example and we clung together, hardly ever leaving the beach, busy with building castles or a wailing wall out of mud.

Later, when a convoy of cars resembling a modern-day wagon train headed out for the hills in America, a new *shtetl* was founded in the Catskill Mountains. The settlement had small cabins surrounding a swimming pool and a rectangular-shaped communal building where we had

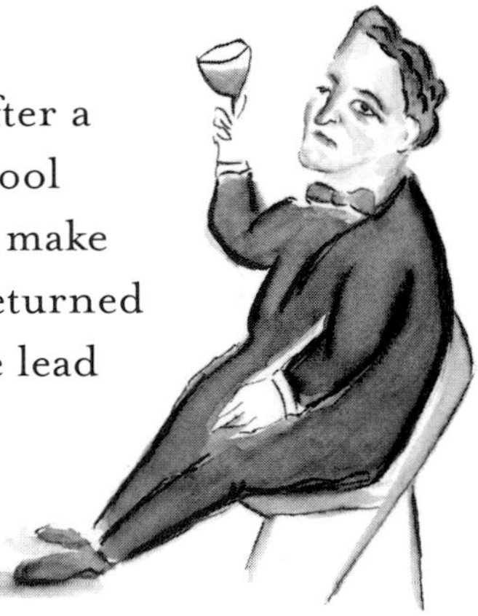

our first taste of bingo and cherry Coke. After a couple of weeks of cannonballing into the pool and picking blueberries for our mothers to make pies, the families packed up, and the cars returned to the road all in a straight line, ours in the lead with my father the wagonmaster.

My parents and their friends would return to these hills many times, leaving their children, once they were teenagers, at home with enough money to order Chinese food every night and look after their parents' businesses. But now, instead of staying in sparsely decorated cabins, they booked in to Grossinger's or Brown's, both popular resorts where other Greenies vacationed. They would now be able to meet other groups. Their horizon had expanded.

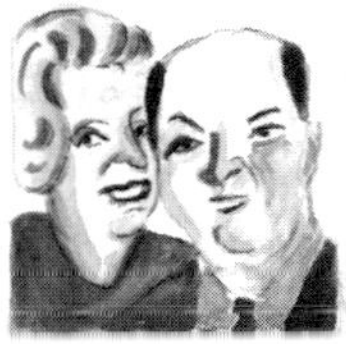

The chance for me to do the same had arisen and I told my mother to call Bluma.

At the end of a very long road and after somehow following my mother's encrypted directions and backtracking several times, we arrived. Although I had never been there before, the colony looked familiar with its tiny cottages tightly packed together in a U shape, with a swimming pool in the middle. It was an ideal retirement plan: winter in a condominium in Florida and return to a cabin in the Borsht Belt, and in both places be in the company of friends.

Bluma had the identifiable appearance of a Group member: straw-blonde hair pouffed high and stiff, which looked exactly the same the next morning when she woke up—truly a miracle. And of course her left arm was tattooed. She walked with an air of determination, her husky body moving solidly forward. Bass-toned and somber, her voice complemented her gait. It was as if sound and motion conveyed the story of her life. She talked about her husband and the war and frequently interrupted herself with, "Dahlink, if I started crying, I would never be able to stop." I had heard these words spoken before, by other members of the Group.

She was very pleased to have our company. Her husband had died not long ago and now her sister, absent from the adjoining cabin, was extremely ill. It was just the beginning of the summer season, and others, like herself, had only recently arrived from Florida. We were in luck: it was a Friday, and that evening there was to be a catered supper and dance held in the communal building, an event Bluma had organized. We would meet the rest of the con- clave that night.

The hall was decorated with streamers and balloons and the men and women had

MY HUSBAND IS VERY SICK NOW. TELL ME, WOULD YOU TAKE HIS PICTURE FOR ME?

taken their fancy clothing out of plastic wrap for the
occasion. Suits and sequins entered the room and the
one-man band, a *tummler*, played Yiddish folk songs and
disco tunes on his accordion. And there we were, line
dancing with seventy-five-year-olds.

I took photographs of people who knew my parents,
some from their hometowns in Poland, others who had
made their acquaintance when they wintered in Florida.

They all extended the same warmth I had received whenever I'd been among my parents' friends. Suddenly, I was a *kindlach* again—albeit an aging one—and I felt the bittersweet pull of *gedenk*, remember, and came to understand in a new way the breadth of its reach. It was as if the word had been silently spoken by a generation soon to be gone—*Remember us*.

When we returned to Toronto, I called my mother to tell her how much I had enjoyed being with her friends, people to whom she had become close over the last few years, wintering in Florida on her own after my father had passed away. But all too soon the tone of our conversation shifted. My mother asked when I would be able to come and visit her, since I had not seen her in a while. I said that I wasn't exactly sure, and she was direct in expressing her displeasure—I wish you made more time to see me. And suddenly I was drawn into the circle of hell belonging to mothers and daughters.

My mother has been without my father for fourteen years and her world grows smaller. After my father died, I promised myself that I would never be the one to end a conversation with my mother, leaving her alone, feeling sad and then more alone. From an early age, I'd learned to keep hurt and disappointment secret from my parents, who always seemed to be looking more to each other and to their friends. Yet when my mother says these things, a strong emotion comes, unbidden. What about me? I have always felt that she and my father never made time for me. *Oy-oy*, I feel like a Jewish yo-yo. Now I'm about eight years

old, then ten, twelve, sixteen, my life flashing before my
eyes. Whatever age I go to, when I look for my parents,
they're off somewhere with their group of friends.

The phone call came to an end and closed as it often
does with my mother and me finding words to bridge
over the moments of potential friction. We have always
wished for the other a pleasant day and said that we will
speak again tomorrow. This time, as if to bring comfort
for something unspoken, and revealing an understanding
of what she has always known about me, she adds, "May
your heart give you peace."

*I have never discovered the Holocaust's
vanishing point, have never been quite sure
where to stand on its horizon.* I had not gone with
my mother and brother on their trip to Auschwitz, but
in 2003 when the Holocaust Museum in Washington,
D.C., invited survivors and children of survivors to
commemorate its tenth anniversary, I knew that I would
attend. My mother wanted to go, but for some reason
I can't remember she was unable to. While I would have
liked to have made this trip with her, I also knew that in
her company it would have been different. I would have
taken in the experience of this gathering through her
eyes and not my own, and possibly had difficulty later
separating my feelings from hers. Perhaps it was time
to stand in front of that truck without protection and
to find balance without any counterweight. But as I
would find, I had been unprepared in some way for
the enormity of what I would see.

The museum had set up a large tent on its grounds where food for seven thousand people was served throughout the day. There were hundreds of tables, on each of which was a stand holding a card printed with a name—Majdanek, Buchenwald, Dachau, Bergen-Belsen, Auschwitz, Bedzin, Lodz. Names of Polish and German towns and concentration camps displayed so that people who had come from those places could grab a Danish and a coffee or fill their paper plates with cold cuts and salad and sit down to eat with people they had not seen for decades, or meet others they had not known before. The scene had a surreality. I went over to "Bergen-Belsen," introduced myself, and asked the group of people seated at that table if any of them had known my parents.

A frail-looking woman stands up and tells me that her name is Bronka Burnbaum. Did you meet my father? Did you know Ben Eisenstein? I see her looking at my face and that she is surprised.

"Your father ran a canteen in Bergen-Belsen after the war. I knew your father well. My husband was his friend. I can see his face now."

I can still see hers and remember that when she let me take her into my arms I'd felt that I had entered a place where time had begun to measure loss and my father had begun to move forward.

Later, I meet another woman and we begin to talk. She asks me a few questions about my parents, where I have come from. I tell her my mother is well, living in Toronto, and that she would have liked to have come.

Then she tells me about the family she lost and of her internment in Auschwitz. As we part, she extends a message: "Say hello to your mother from Auschwitz." Greetings conveyed through me from one woman to another, women who will never meet.

WISHING EVERYONE A HAPPY HEALTHY NEW YEAR, FROM BERGEN-BELSEN, 1947.

I spend the rest of the afternoon in the museum, which eloquently guides its visitors through the story of the Holocaust. There is overwhelming information to read: dates, European-Jewish populations of towns before the war, after the war, numbers, numbing numbers. Scaling the walls of a three-story passageway are countless

images of people—the ultimate Group—who had lived
in Eishishok, a small Lithuanian town. These photographs
are the remnants of a nine-hundred-year-old Jewish
community wiped out within two days in 1941. This is
not a place of hope and impossible to leave.

As I walked through room after room of carefully
displayed and documented history, I was surrounded
by a world in which order could not be found. The past
my parents had lived through was all around me.

I had always felt that if I could find my parents' deepest hurt I could locate my own grief, for them. But how
could I have ever imagined that everything the Holocaust
had voided in their lives could be replaced, as if my need
to understand could somehow make up for such sorrow.
I will never be able to know the truth of what my parents
had experienced. It is beyond my reach, and perhaps
even theirs, to know the full extent of their loss.

There is one more room to enter, the Hall of
Remembrance. This is a place for silent contemplation,
where a memorial candle can be lit. Its concrete walls
are engraved with the names of concentration camps,
and there is an inscription, words that have presided
over the centuries.

Only guard yourself and guard your soul carefully,
lest you forget the things your eyes saw, and lest
these things depart your heart all the days of your
life, and you shall make them known to your
children, and to your children's children.

—Deuteronomy 4:9

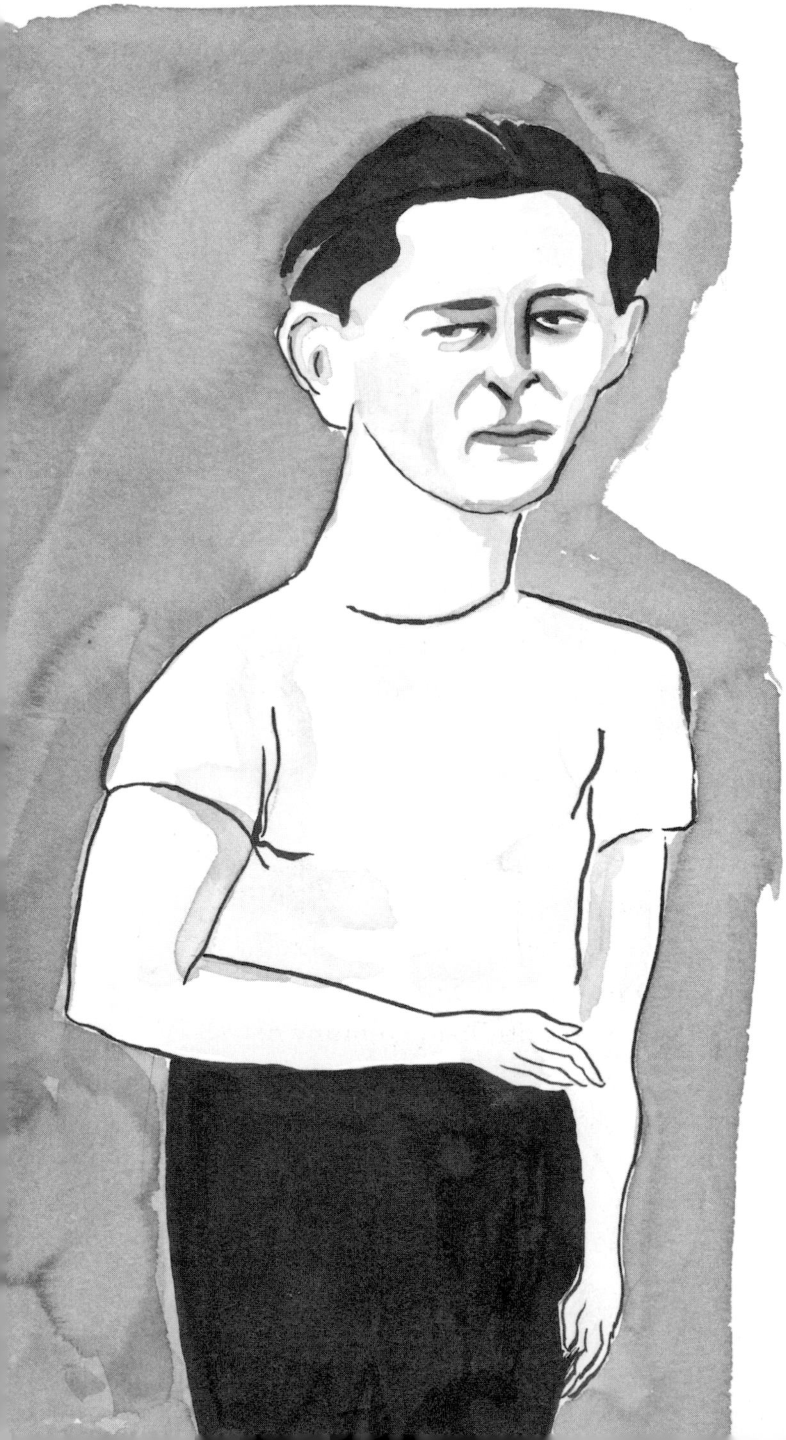

A Naming

The day a child is born holds all the potential for the life that will be; the day of death is the completion for who we have become. Both need attending, first to welcome entry and then finally to receive what has been left behind.

When my son was born, just months after my father died, he was circumcised and named in our house on the eighth day after his birth. Our living room was small and it filled with our friends and family, who had gathered to welcome a boy into his community, one generation connecting to the next through the traditional ceremony of the *bris*.

My son was carried into the room, wearing a small crocheted *yarmulke* on his fuzzy head, draped in the tiniest *tallis* ever made, and sucking on a cotton swab that had been dipped in wine, the original anesthetic drip. When his foreskin was cut, he cried a pure cry. Then, in the traditional way, my son was given his name, Ben, and then his Hebrew name, Dov.

During the ceremony, as a word from a ghostly world was spoken and retrieved, friends circled tightly around my family to celebrate a child's entry into Jewish life, their presence reminding me of the last time they had gathered, to observe the rituals of burial on the occasion of my father's death.

There is no center to be found in memory, but each place holds its heartbeat.

My father had not been feeling well for a few months. He went to the hospital to have some tests, and later the attending doctor took us aside. We were unprepared for the diagnosis we heard. The doctor told us that cancer had been found, that it had already spread like brushfire throughout his body, and there was very little time left to him. How little remained for us.

It took only two weeks for my father to die. There were moments during that time when, at five months pregnant, I was unable to imagine that once I had watched my father's life end, a new life would soon after be placed into my arms. Every night, my mother slept in the empty hospital bed next to him. Sharon and Michael shared with her my father's last fitful long nights. My family, concerned that I get some rest, had convinced me that it would be better if I did not stay. Throughout those days, the continual visits of friends and family members were accompanied by constant vigil and the sense of impossibility that his life could be taken from us so suddenly.

There was an elderly gentleman on the same floor who lived nearby in my parents' neighborhood and was an acquaintance of theirs, a fellow countryman from Europe. Every day, he strolled down the hall to my father's room, pushing his IV alongside. He always came in, quietly inquiring as to how my father was doing. During the last hours of my father's life, this dignified frail man appeared in the doorway. You can't come in now, Ben is dying. And the man was gone.

My father died that morning and the day somehow continued without him. The funeral was held the following afternoon and he was buried in a Jewish cemetery at the north end of the city, where several of his friends had already been laid to rest. After the funeral, we returned to my parents' home, now the *shivah* house for the next seven days. The living room and dining room were overcrowded with family and friends who had come to give condolence, and the expressions of sorrow combined with a feeling of disbelief.

The table had been laid out with bagels and lox, herring, cream cheese, fruit, and an assortment of cakes and cookies for guests, reminding everyone that in the presence of death, life is sustained. The immediate family sat together on low chairs or stools or on the couch with the cushions removed, signifying that we had been brought low, reduced through grief. Throughout the length of the *shivah*, the mourner's Kaddish was recited twice daily, once before the approach of sundown and then after sunrise, and at those times the house was at its fullest with the friends of my parents.

I remember that on the last evening, just after the Kaddish had been recited, I realized that the prayer was to be chanted only once more, the next morning, and that the initial period of loss shared communally would come to a close. I was sitting on the couch—cushionless and uncomfortable—between my brother and sister, my mother next to her. At one point, we looked up and saw the gentleman from the hospital standing before us, and I sensed the sad symmetry of having his presence once again at a final moment. This man, whom I had never really met, belonged in our home on this night, on the eve of the *shivah* coming to a close. He had come to pay his respects. He was dressed in a fine suit and looked well. I had no recollection of his entering the room or leaving it, only that he was briefly there. This man we hardly knew had walked around the periphery of our loss, yet his attendance had been marked, his solemnity accepted, and I was reminded of the tales in Jewish legend about the *Lamed-vav*, the Unknown Just Men. In every generation, thirty-six men are chosen by God to carry the sorrows of the world. Ordinary men, indistinguishable from other men, unknown to one another.

My father knew that he was dying even though the doctors never told him directly. The knowledge was there in his eyes. Once, a friend called long distance from Florida, having heard that he was ill,

and when my mother spoke into the phone and said that
he was being treated, my father yelled across the room,
"Tell them I'm dying."

The one day my grandparents came to visit him, they
were not attentive to him or to their daughter's imminent
loss, as if all they could see in my dying father was what
awaited them. And when the doctor arrived, making his
daily rounds, Moishe and Machele *krechtsed* and moaned
of their own pains, so I asked them to leave, told them to
go home.

My aunt Jenny came to visit regularly with her determined air of hopefulness, an optimism that would burn
itself out in five years' time when she would care tirelessly
for her own husband, making health-food concoctions
that he would eat without appetite just to please her. She
tried encouraging my father to exercise, to sit up and
breathe deeply, so that more oxygen would flow through
his body. She didn't have a blender with her or else she
would have mixed up some $H2O$ and broccoli and fed it
through his intravenous line in the hope that the cancer
eroding my father's body would take a break and eat:
Ess, ess, mein kind.

Every day, I would visit my father and sit next to him,
standing at the foot of his bed when others came to see
him or walking from his room to the elevator and back,
counting the steps it took. On the night that would be
his last, I got up to leave and leaned close to my father.
My mother was sitting in a chair with her eyes closed but
I knew she was not asleep, she had not been able to rest
for nearly two weeks. As I kissed my father goodnight,

he turned his head to look at me. In his eyes, dimness had now replaced a vibrant clarity. After a moment, he lifted his hand and placed it gently on my stomach and said, "You are carrying my name."

The next morning, we watched my father drown. In turn, Michael, Sharon, and I went close to his ear and whispered our love. I listened to my aunt wail her devotion, her song of farewell to my father, knowing then that I had not before understood the extent of her feelings. My uncle stood quietly for hours, silent in his acceptance as his brother died. I see them as entwined—my mother, father, aunt, and uncle. More than I could know was being lost. My mother's sorrow poured out while she and her sister touched my father's face and arms, as if they were the tide flowing over him. When stillness entered the room, my mother and aunt combed his hair, washed him, preparing his body according to Jewish tradition— their final caress before my father's body would be taken from us.

On the day of my son's bris, my mother came to our house early in the morning to help my husband, John, and me set the table with food before the arrival of guests. She wanted to have some time with her granddaughter, Anna, to hold her new grandson, and to be alone with me and all that we felt this day had brought together for our family.

She knew I was quite nervous about the circumcision and, in her offhand reassurance—"*Oy*, don't worry, it's quick. The baby will already be *shikker*, drunk, from the taste of wine"—I took some comfort, but then asked her why my breasts were filled only with milk. We both laughed, and then she suggested that I rest for a little while because everyone would be arriving soon and most likely at the same time. Which they did.

When the ceremony began, as is customary, my daughter and I stood off to the side along with the other women in the room. This meant that I did not actually have to watch the circumcision that would be performed by the *mohel*. The men in the room crowded around the baby, in small part, I think, curious to catch sight of what they had once drunkenly missed, now able to witness and honor the event that had first linked them to their heritage, to their origins in an ancient world.

My son cried briefly, and then my brother lifted his nephew and placed him into the arms of his father, who held him as he was named.

O you dig and I dig,
    and I dig towards you,
and on our finger
    the ring awakes.

— PAUL CELAN

Acknowledgments

A final page to express gratitude and to thank those who have given their support and encouragement in the writing of this book.

There is a Yiddish saying: The light of a candle is useful when it precedes you. To Ellen Seligman of McClelland & Stewart, my publisher and editor, whose vision and passion illuminated the way. It is impossible to convey the extent of the dedication and care she gave to the manuscript from its development through to its completion. Her touch is felt on every page. This book would not be what it is without her wisdom and guidance, and her capacity to understand hidden truths.

To others at McClelland & Stewart, for making a publishing house a home. My thanks to Doug Pepper, for his warm reception to the book. To Marilyn Biderman, for placing the manuscript into the hands of international publishers, and for personally embracing the book. To Anita Chong, for her grace and professionalism, and her help. And also to Krista Willis, Vicki Black, Bruce Walsh, Ruta Liormonas, and Heather Sangster.

To my agent, Dean Cooke—a *mensh*—and Suzanne Brandreth, for their ongoing support.

Thank you to Michel Vrána who planted the seed of design and to Tania Craan who made it bloom.

To my publishers and editors outside Canada, including Ursula Doyle, Picador, UK; Robbert Ammerlaan, De Bezige Bij, Holland; Megan Lynch, Riverhead/Penguin Group, US; Luigi Brioschi, Guanda, Italy; Francis Geffard, Albin Michel, France; Mónica Carmona, Random House Mondadori, Spain—thank you. I would also like to acknowledge Cindy Spiegel, formerly of Riverhead, for her important early support in the acquisition of the book.

And finally, to my family. To my father and mother, to my sister, Sharon, and my brother, Michael. To Anna and Ben, and to John, the center of my heartbeat.

$\sim$

are from "Der Alter Tzigayner" by Abraham Ellstein and Jacob Jacobs. Copyright © 1942 (Renewed) by Music Sales Corporation. Used by permission of Music Sales Corporation. The lines by Paul Celan on page 189 are from the poem "There was earth inside them," from *Poems of Paul Celan*, translated by Michael Hamburger. Translation copyright © 1972, 1980, 1988, 2002 by Michael Hamburger. Used by permission of Persea Books.

Quotes in the drawing that follows the dedication page: Charlotte Salomon: from *To Paint Her Life: Charlotte Salomon in the Nazi Era* by Mary Lowenthal Felstiner (HarperCollins, 1994); Bruno Schulz: from *Letters and Drawings of Bruno Schulz*, edited by Jerzy Ficowski (Harper and Row, 1988); Hannah Arendt: from a letter written to Gershom Scholem, July 24, 1963, in *Scholem, Arendt, Klemperer: Intimate Chronicles in Turbulent Times* by Steven E. Aschheim (Indiana University Press, 2001); Elie Wiesel: from *All Rivers Run to the Sea* by Elie Wiesel (Knopf, 1995); Primo Levi: from *The Voice of Memory: Interviews, 1961-1987*, edited by Marco Belpoliti and Robert Gordon (The New Press, 2001).

Line on page 65: "Heaven will know and God will remember" is from *The Joys of Yiddish* by Leo Rosten (Pocket Books, Simon and Schuster, 1968). On page 82: words that appear in the panel drawing of Adolf Eichmann are taken from a statement he made as quoted by Simon Wiesenthal in the documentary *The Yellow Star: The Persecution of the Jews in Europe 1933-45* by Dieter Hildebrandt; Hannah Arendt's statement is from her posthumously published lecture collection, *The Life of the Mind* (Harcourt Brace Jovanovich, 1978); Primo Levi's words are from *The Voice of Memory*. On page 160: lyrics quoted are from the traditional Romanian folk song "Basarabye." The Bergen-Belsen New Year's card on page 177 was drawn from *Holocaust and Rebirth*, edited by Sam E. Bloch (Bergen-Belsen Memorial Press, 1965).

For Yiddish spelling, I have occasionally used *A Dictionary of Yiddish Slang and Idioms* by Fred Kogos (Castle Books, 1966), but mainly I have relied upon Leo Rosten's transliterations, in *The Joys of Yiddish*, since his spellings of words and phrases are as my heart and ear remember the language I first heard.

A NOTE ON THE TYPE

The body text is set in Mrs Eaves, a typeface designed in 1996 by Zuzana Licko, as a reinterpretation of the eighteenth-century Baskerville typeface. Noted for its fanciful ligatures and reminiscent of customized lettering, the font is named after Sarah Eaves, John Baskerville's housekeeper and later his wife. Licko and her husband, Rudy VanderLans, co-founded *Emigre* magazine in 1984, which received increased recognition when it began to incorporate Licko's digital type designs.

The cursive display font is Dear Sarah and was designed in 2004 by Christian Robertson.

The font that accompanies the drawings is Litterbox. Recognized for its playfulness and vigor, it was designed in 1995 by Calgary artist Dean Stanton.